The Future of China's Past

SUNY series in Chinese Philosophy and Culture
―――――――
Roger T. Ames, editor

The Future of China's Past

Reflections on the Meaning of China's Rise

ALBERT WELTER

Published by State University of New York Press, Albany

© 2023 State University of New York

All rights reserved

Printed in the United States of America

No part of this book may be used or reproduced in any manner whatsoever without written permission. No part of this book may be stored in a retrieval system or transmitted in any form or by any means including electronic, electrostatic, magnetic tape, mechanical, photocopying, recording, or otherwise without the prior permission in writing of the publisher.

For information, contact State University of New York Press, Albany, NY
www.sunypress.edu

Library of Congress Cataloging-in-Publication Data

Name: Welter, Albert, 1952– author.
Title: The future of China's past : reflections on the meaning of China's rise / Albert Welter.
Other titles: Reflections on the meaning of China's rise
Description: Albany, New York : State University of New York Press, [2023] | Series: SUNY series in Chinese philosophy and culture | Includes bibliographical references and index.
Identifiers: LCCN 2022021048 | ISBN 9781438491677 (hardcover : alk. paper) | ISBN 9781438491684 (ebook) | ISBN 9781438491660 (pbk. : alk. paper)
Subjects: LCSH: China—Civilization—21st century. | China—Forecasting.
Classification: LCC DS779.43 .W45 2023 | DDC 951.06—dc23/eng/20220520
LC record available at https://lccn.loc.gov/2022021048

10 9 8 7 6 5 4 3 2 1

Contents

List of Illustrations	vii
Preface	ix
Introduction China and the East Asian Renaissance, Toward a New World Order	1
Chapter One The Return of the Native: The Fall and Rise of Confucius in Modern China	17
Chapter Two Chinese Authoritarianism: The Role of Legalism and Militarism in the Making of Modern China	41
Chapter Three The Daoist Cycle of Life and the Way of Returning to the Fundamental: Millenarian Prophecy and the Environmental Movement in Contemporary China	59
Chapter Four The Return of the Nonnative: The Buddhist Revival in Contemporary China	75
Chapter Five Back to the Future? Prospects for Confucianism and Chinese Traditions in Contemporary China	101

CONCLUDING REFLECTIONS	119
EPILOGUE	129
POSTSCRIPT	133
NOTES	139
FURTHER READING	151
INDEX	155

Illustrations

Figures

1.1 Venerating Confucius at Boston University, September 30, 2018, 2,569th anniversary of Confucius's birth.   20

1.2 A bronze statue of Confucius is pictured in front of the National Museum of China on Tiananmen Square in Beijing, China, January 11, 2011.   30

1.3 Xi Jinping addressing the fifth Congress of the International Confucian Association in the Great Hall of the People, September 24, 2014.   32

2.1 Four Classes according to Confucianism.   42

2.2 Dynastic cycle in China. Author provided.   48

3.1 Diagram of the working of the Dao.   65

3.2 A monumental statue at Mt. Qingyuan of Lao-Tzu, the Chinese philosopher who lived c. 500 BCE and who is credited with founding Daoism (Taosim).   70

4.1 "All erroneous ideas, all poisonous weeds, all ghosts and monsters, must be subjected to criticism; in no circumstance should they be allowed to spread unchecked."   80

4.2 King Aśoka Stūpa in Ningbo, China.   84

4.3 King Aśoka style stūpa unearthed from Leifeng Pagoda ruins.   86

4.4	Yanshou Stūpa, Hangzhou, China, with circumambulating worshippers.	88
4.5	Leifeng Pagoda stakeholders.	90
4.6	Budai Maitreya statue at Xuedou Monastery in Ningbo.	93
5.1	Ding vessel, Late Shang Dynasty, Shanghai Museum.	116
5.2	The Chinese Communist Party (after Jarrod Fankhauser, ABC News, posted March 5, 2019).	116
5.3	Contemporary authoritarian model of Socialism with Chinese Characteristics (inclusion of traditions/religions).	117
P.1	Territorial demarcations associated with Han civilization.	135

Table

5.1	Responses to Creating Cultural (Wen) Models in the Early Song Dynasty	104

Preface

I tend to get asked two different kinds of questions regarding my work: Americans ask me how I got interested in China; Chinese ask how I got interested in Buddhism. I tell Americans about how I stumbled upon China as an undergraduate student and became fascinated with its history and culture. Before I knew it, I was studying Chinese with a particular interest in China's premodern intellectual traditions. From that time on, I have always felt that the humanities were diminished without China's long, rich legacy of contributions.

As for the Chinese, we all know that religion can be a touchy subject in China, less so these days than before but still needing some delicacy at times. I recall my first time traveling to China in the early 1980s and being encircled on the Bund in Shanghai by a crowd of a hundred or more curious Chinese, wondering who the *laowai* (foreigner) was in their recently opened but still mostly forbidden land. When they learned that I had come to study Buddhism, a nervous hush fell over the crowd. My Chinese interlocutor for the group, an "elderly" gentleman ("elderly" being a relative term, as I have come to find almost forty years later) quickly asked me a few clarifying questions about the nature of my study and was able to announce to the palpable relief of the crowd that I was *"biàn zhèng wéi wù zhǔ yì zhě"* (a "dialectical materialist"). In a country that at the time was very committed to Marxism both in theory and in application, being a dialectical materialist—one who studied religious forces from a social-scientific, nonconfessional perspective—was definitely a good thing. The day was saved (and so was I).

This book began as a course with a similar title for the Humanities Seminar Program (HSP) at the University of Arizona in fall 2018. The Humanities Seminar Program is a distinctive opportunity for academics to showcase their work for a dedicated group of seminarians, mostly comprising retired professionals residing either permanently or temporarily in the Tucson area, taking advantage of southern Arizona's pleasant winter temperatures. The HSP draws an accomplished crowd, far more experienced and engaging than the typical undergraduate class. HSP seminarians have enjoyed successful careers in business, economics, politics, health professions, the judiciary, city planning, publishing, and academia, etc. Courses are solicited from tenured faculty across the university, ranging in disciplinary expertise but tending toward humanities-related content.

Professors who teach in the HSP typically adopt a course they have taught in the undergraduate curriculum for years. Somewhat foolishly, I failed to follow this example and decided to branch out to explore a new topic, one I was interested in but had not taught previously. As most first ventures, it was not without hiccups; however, most of the ninety or so seminarians braved the ten-week course with me. A few of them even suggested that I turn the course material into a book. Stealing whatever free time I had away from administrative and teaching duties, in addition to an active scholarly schedule that includes regular conference and other academic presentations, I whittled down the number of topics to the most salient and drafted several chapters. The result is before you now. I am grateful to all the HSP seminarians for their interest in the topic and the questions and comments they provided that helped refine my ideas, which were in various stages of development. I am especially grateful to Jerome West and Ron Engel, both of whom contributed to the shape of the book in significant ways. Nancy Green was kind enough to offer her editorial skills to the project, and as a result, typos, errors, and other infelicitous turns of phrase have been all but eliminated. Any that remain are the sole responsibility of the author. I would also like to thank the HSP directors and staff who helped facilitate the course, and the dean of the College of Humanities, Alain-Philippe Durand, who invited me to put forth a proposal. I am also grateful to Roger Ames for including the volume in the SUNY series in Chinese Philosophy and Culture.

Like the HSP class itself, the book is not intended for professional Sinologists and academics working in areas related to Chinese studies but for an educated and interested lay public who are seeking ways to understand China and the possibilities it represents. There is a lot here for a nonspecialist to absorb, but my hope is that the presentation is engaging, logical, and thought-provoking so as to provide an avenue into the world of China and the prospects that it portends for its own as well as our futures. While I strongly believe in the need for a book such as this that addresses the topic of China's rise and its current retrieval of tradition, I am not necessarily the only, or even the best person to take up the task. Where I have fallen short, I invite others join in and continue the dialogue. For those who disagree with some aspect I have chosen, I remind them of the immensity of China and the diversity it represents, both past and present. There is room for differing perspectives and a need to address them.

Introduction

China and the East Asian Renaissance, Toward a New World Order

Introduction

As we enter the third decade of the twenty-first century, it is clear that the Western-led liberal international order established after the Second World War is coming to some kind of end. Or, at the very least, it is transitioning into something else yet to be defined but incredibly crucial for the future of the planet. As with all crucial transitions, this one demands all the interpretative resources we can bring to it. Many contributors bring expertise on economic and international relations and power analyses, but in the present case, cultural, religious, ethical, and historical analyses are needed as well. These may play a much more important role in the new era than generally estimated.

China's rise may be the single most transformative event of our times. Many have called attention to the economic impact of China's rise, but it is in itself not unprecedented and must be seen in the larger context of an Asian economic renaissance. Beginning in the late nineteenth century, Japan forged a new consensus that served as an inspiration and model for the non-Western world and demonstrated how Western industrialization and technology could be successfully adapted beyond the Euro-American sphere. This model, under the rubric of "Eastern ethics/morality, Western technical learning" (*tōyō dōtoku, seiyō gakugei*), a slogan coined by politician, scholar, and Japanese reformer Sakuma Shōzan, proved particularly inspirational throughout Asia. A similar model was attempted in Late Qing dynasty China under the rubric of *ti* and *yong*, essence and function, whereby China could preserve its spiritual core while adopting Western scientific and technological innovations. It is discussed in more detail below.

In spite of the failure of the Japanese imperial mission that imagined an Asia free of Western colonialisms under the banner of "Asia for Asians," the rest of Asia was eventually enticed to follow Japan's lead in adopting a modernity based on Western models. Following the economic success of the "four tigers," Taiwan, South Korea, Hong Kong, and Singapore, and the rapid economic advancement of Southeast Asia, especially since the end of the cold war, this model became pervasive throughout Asia (with the exception of North Korea) by the end of the twentieth century.

Japan's method for dealing with Western intrusions was not isolated. Around the same time, the Qing government in China devised a plan known as the Self-Strengthening Movement to acquire and utilize Western methods under the slogan, "Learn barbarian methods to combat barbarian threats." This initiative followed China's humiliating defeats in the Opium Wars that exposed China's military and technological weaknesses. Confronted with superior British forces fortified by developments following the industrial revolution, Chinese weaknesses were exposed. While the Self-Strengthening Movement produced some successful capitalist and military reforms, most of these were locally based and failed to garner national support from the Qing government. Qing leaders adhered to a pattern that would come to characterize many indigenous movements that aspired to military and economic modernization without accompanying social or political reforms. In this, they invoked a pattern with a long history in China and throughout East Asia, the essence/function (*ti/yong*) matrix. This matrix differentiates reality in terms of two aspects, an absolute aspect, the fundamental cause or origin, and a relative aspect, the concrete manifestation of the essence in contemporary realities. The *ti/yong* model was invoked as a way to preserve a hypothetically essential cultural identity in the face of rampant change from external factors. "Learning barbarian methods to combat barbarian threats" was a strategy aimed at acquiring Western technical learning in order to preserve an Eastern moral spirit. Combining Western superiority in science and technology with the East's superior moral spirit would allegedly result in an unbeatable formula for deterring military intrusions from the West while preserving the East's cultural autonomy. Key to the model's success was an ability to remain uncontaminated by perceived Western spiritual deficiencies while acquiring its scientific acumen, guarding against spiritual pollution from Western ways of thinking while adopting its superior technology.

China (and East Asia) posed little threat while the region was on the defensive, absorbed in acquiring Western technologies while attempting to preserve cultural autonomy. Western leaders flattered themselves with the superiority of Western learning, political, social, and economic institutions. Modernity itself, in this view, was a product of the West, and its manifestations, in whatever garb, were intrinsically predicated on normative assumptions developed in the European enlightenment. This may be likened to a Western version of a *ti/yong* matrix, whereby an essential Western way of thinking, exhibited through the culture of science and technology, functions in various guises according to cultural context.

This Western version of a *ti/yong* model that considers Western thinking as essential and Chinese thought as peripheral has also occurred in the modern Chinese context. Chinese scholar, philosopher, and intellectual historian Li Zehou, for example, emerged as a central figure of the Chinese Enlightenment of the 1980s. In the wake of Deng Xiaoping's reforms and economic opening, Li's search for a new model for China combined elements from Western philosophy—especially Karl Marx's analysis of materialistic and historical realities in the evolution of human societies and Immanuel Kant's view of the intellectual, moral, and aesthetic capacities of the individual—with key components drawn from the Chinese philosophical tradition. His impact on the generation of Chinese emerging from the nightmares of the Cultural Revolution was profound. Yu Ying-shih, a prominent Chinese intellectual historian at Princeton University, commented that Li's books "emancipated a whole generation of young Chinese intellectuals from Communist ideology."[1] In a famous 1987 essay, Li turned conventional Chinese (and East Asian) thinking on its head, declaring that "the Western is the Substance, and the Chinese is for Application," with "substance" being an alternate translation for *ti*, and "application" an alternate for *yong*.[2] According to Li, the technology and conceptual frameworks of the West comprise the root or substance of modernity, including Chinese modernity, and Chinese cultural adaptations can only serve as applications, influencing but not dictating the core. In the wake of the Tiananmen Square protests of 1989, Li was labeled a "thought criminal" and placed under house arrest. He eventually received permission to travel to the United States, where he was granted asylum. Regardless of Li's ultimate impact on the course of Chinese thinking, his rebuttal to the *ti/yong* hypothesis is a pertinent reminder of the state of flux that modern Chinese thinking has undergone and continues to undergo, pushed between the pillars of Marxism, Western liberal ideas, and traditional Chinese ways of thinking.

What happens when China is no longer on the defensive? We had a prelude, of sorts, to this in the 1980s when Japan reached an economic pinnacle amid assertions like Ezra Vogel's provocative title, *Japan as Number One*,[3] and the impending era of Japanese economic dominance. By the late 1980s, before the period of Japan's economic stagnation set in and when a trade war with Japan was threatening to burst into full bloom, it was fashionable in Tokyo to talk of an evolution of the world order in terms of paradigm shifts: *Pax Romana, Pax Britannica, Pax Americana*, and the imminent *Pax Japonica*. Japan's posturing eventually gave way to the realities of the market, and to a steady realization that Japan was tied to the economic and political world order in ways that threatened to do lasting damage should it decide to go its own way. Decades of tutelage under the United States and the liberal democratic order (e.g., the United Nations, World Bank, etc.) instituted after the Second World War predetermined Japan's integration into this economic and political world order.

There are similarities between China's situation and Japan's in the 1980s, but there are significant differences as well. Most importantly, China did not experience decades of tutelage from the United States and the liberal democratic order following the Second World War. While China has been integrated to some extent into the economic and political world order in recent decades, it remains to be seen if these ties are valuable enough to China to forgo independent initiatives, or whether China is strong enough to go its own way and fashion a new economic and political order. Recent developments, like the Belt and Road Initiative (BRI),[4] the Asian Infrastructure Investment Bank (AIIB),[5] and China's important role in the Shanghai Cooperation Organization (SCO),[6] suggest such initiatives. Beyond this, Japan is a country with a population of roughly 125 million people (and falling), while China comprises more than ten times that total, roughly 1.4 billion people. China's 2017 GNP was 23.24 trillion US dollars. Japan's was 5.765 trillion US dollars, and the US GNP was 19.61 trillion dollars for the same period. In comparison, the United States had a 5.923 trillion US dollar GNP in 1990 compared to Japan's at 2.423 trillion. By any measure, Japan's GNP was fractional compared with the United States. China, buoyed by its overwhelming population, has surpassed the United States in GNP. While GDP per capita figures still overwhelmingly favor the United States (surpassing $59,000 in 2017; China remained a little under $9,000), the point is that China with its overwhelming population, production capacity, and foreign reserves, not to mention its decades (centuries if one considers Chinese history as a whole) of experience outside the liberal democratic world order, represents a far bigger challenge to the world order than Japan ever could. Given China's long history and dynastic cycles of prosperity and decline, it is considered a given among Chinese and China watchers that China is destined to rise again and resume its natural status as a leading regional and international force. The dynastic cycle, considered in more detail in chapter 3, offers an indigenous, traditional explanation of the forces that generate political authority, economic prosperity, and social well-being, as well as the factors that lead to decline and ultimate demise. It posits the state as an organic unit functioning symbiotically with political, economic, and social forces through cycles of rise and fall, governed by a concept known as the Mandate of Heaven. According to this process, rule in China is not arbitrary but is a function of Heaven's will, or mandate. Heaven here is a divine force that determines the natural order inscribed in the operation of the universe. Those who rule do so by virtue of Heaven's approval. The rule of a dynasty persists so long as rulers maintain their virtue, signaled by Heaven's approval, exhibited in the prosperity and peace of society. As prosperity and peace decline, Heaven's approval is withdrawn. Social upheaval ensues and political rebellion occurs. The mandate is revoked and passed on to a new ruler, who initiates a new dynasty and social order, ushering in a new regime of peace and prosperity.

The long span of Chinese history and the continuity of Chinese cultural motifs offer a perspective on the process of cyclical change that is not easily detectable elsewhere. Within the microanalysis of cyclical dynastic change covering China's traditionally recognized twenty-four dynasties dating back to the second millennium BCE if not before, there are periods recognized not only for their evolution of existing patterns but as groundbreaking paradigm shifts that break with the old and usher in the new. Up until the early twentieth century, two such periods are recognized: the end of the Warring States period and advent of the Qin and Han dynasties in the third century BCE, as well as the fall of the Tang and advent of the Song dynasty in the tenth century CE. The paradigm initiated in the Song lasted through the Qing dynasty, the last imperial dynasty, when its presuppositions were shattered by Western interventions in the nineteenth century. Since that time, China has been in the throes of seeking a new model for Chinese civilization, a paradigm suitable for China that transcends the limitations of the past and poises China for future greatness. The question of how China reinvents itself—what form or forms China's reassertion of its new paradigm might take—is at the heart of this book.

China has poised itself to forgo its long modern history of being on the defensive and to take an offensive strategy in forging a world order in its image and likeness. As the superiority of China's functional manifestations grow—its industrial capacity, buoyed by a growing scientific, technological, and military confidence—how will China translate this offensive into the cultural arena, to champion the superiority of its indigenous essence, the spirit of China's traditional cultures? As China positions itself as an economic and political leader in world affairs, what role will China's cultural renaissance take? How will this cultural renaissance manifest itself, and what does it bode for the future? As this turn of events unfolds into a new reality, the rise of China (and East Asia generally) forces us to ask questions, many of which are perplexing and challenge some long-held assumptions.

For centuries, since the European Enlightenment, industrialization, and establishment of a world economic order built on European empires and their colonies, the primacy of the West has been assumed. This primacy has been so implicit that it has assumed normative status. Western ideas, institutions, conventions, and standards of behavior and dress have been adopted almost universally around the globe. What happens when this normative status is challenged or revoked? What happens when the primacy of the West—economic, political, and cultural—is questioned? Or are Western ideas so entrenched in notions of modernity that China is unable to alter them? A premise of the current volume is that as solid as the Western bases of modernity are, they are not unalterable and that China is determined to change the model, or at least reassign the pieces that construct it in significant ways.

One of the sacrosanct assumptions of modern capitalism is that market freedoms are inevitably tied to political freedoms. As China attempts to forge its brand of capitalist economic development with the increasing success of a so-called state-sponsored capitalism, what happens to an essential assumption that modern capitalism was built upon?

As a corollary to the above, one of the assumptions of the European version of modernity stemming from the enlightenment is the sanctity of the individual and the role of individual rights and freedoms. The whole nexus of modernity is predicated on the self-evident truths inherent in the individual, endowed with certain inalienable rights. Creativity and innovation, the wellspring of scientific discovery, are necessitated by the individual's inalienable rights and freedoms. What does it mean to foster creativity and innovation outside these parameters? More pointedly, can it be accomplished outside the protections afforded by individual freedom?

One of the political questions that the rise of China poses for a new world order is the specter of authoritarian rule. The current world order has been predicated on democracy and democratic institutions. How would China, with its apparent distaste for democracy and the rights of individuals, alter institutional arrangements in a future civilization predicated on authoritarian rule?

The reputation of Confucianism, long a code word for the Chinese tradition itself, suffered seemingly irreparable damage in the twentieth century for its identification with traditions and customs that inhibited China's ability to modernize. Vilified during the Cultural Revolution as China's nemesis and the font of old and outmoded habits and superstitions, and drawing from themes articulated in the New Cultural movement decades earlier, Confucius has been miraculously revived by the Communist Party as a moral exemplar whose values are compatible with those of the Party itself. What does this cultural counter-revolution bode for the future role of Confucianism in China and the Chinese Communist Party (CCP)? The Confucian revival has also coincided with a return of other Chinese religious and intellectual traditions. What of the future roles of the also once-vilified traditions of Buddhism and Daoism, whose temples and institutions have experienced a remarkable resurgence?

The return of Confucianism, Buddhism, and Daoism to a measure of respectability, if not outright prominence, suggests that their teachings and practices are assuming a role among contemporary Chinese people that had hitherto been restricted, often severely, in the communist era. As this measure of respectability grows and as these traditions reassert their roles in the religious and social lives of the people, one must ask about the role of Marxist ideology in China and the future of "socialism with Chinese characteristics" (as Chinese interpretations and adaptations of the Marxist model are referred to)?

The world is now well aware of the threats posed by climate change and growing environmental degradation. China, to be sure, has been identified as a major culprit in this growing threat. What role will China play in meeting these environmental challenges? Official CCP policy aims at China becoming an Ecological Civilization (*shengtai wenming*). More broadly, as the Chinese embrace new technologies, what role will technology play in their daily lives? How will a future Chinese civilization embrace technology, particularly as a tool of authoritarian control?

Finally, if a new world order is in the offing and China plays a determinative role in formulating this order, it raises the question of what the future will look like. If this future deviates from the past as much as some suggest, it portends a major paradigm shift that will affect many of our habits of thought and what passes for "normative" behavior. The past, including the last few centuries, will be open to reinterpretation in line with a new reality. Whoever controls the future controls the memory of the past as well. Those in the future will write and rewrite the histories of our past to reinforce their contemporary values. The values of individual freedom and expression that were once sacrosanct may be subject to reinterpretation.

It is useful to remember that while China is an old civilization possessing the longest continuous record of any human culture, it is but a young modern nation, dating from 1949. China's attempt at modern reinvention has been a long, often devastating process extending over nearly two hundred years. During this period, characterized as the "century of humiliation," China suffered repeatedly at the hands of Western imperial powers and Japan, punctuated by defeat in the First Opium War (1839–42) and the victory of the Communist Party (1949). During this long, often dark night, China has gone through a prolonged period of self-questioning. What is China? What does it stand for? The most recent period of reexamination is but the latest in a long history of attempts to come to terms with itself and what it means to be Chinese in terms of both its national integrity and its international stature. These debates in China are not new but have a history that predates the People's Republic. The CCP is one outcome of these debates, but even it is an amorphous political conglomerate subject to conflicting tendencies. The return of Confucianism and Chinese traditions to the public square represent a vivid about-face, of sorts, in China's modern trajectory. This is what makes it so fascinating and perplexing. What it means is open to speculation—only future developments will decide how momentous the return of China's past will be for its future. China itself is learning and experimenting with what it is, what it might be. As we explore the dimensions of future possibilities tied to China's past traditions, we will do well to keep in mind the fluidity of current discourses. The novelty of our engagement is second only to that facing the Chinese people themselves, to whom dimensions of their traditions remain a mystery that they are still rediscovering.

Aim of this Book

The current book took shape as a result of the questions that China's rise invite and the need to bring these to a larger forum for discussion. For reasons suggested above, it is incumbent on us to take China's rise seriously, a task for which many are woefully unprepared. This book assumes that perspectives involving modern and contemporary geopolitical and intrastate dynamics are insufficient, on their own, for answering questions regarding China's rise. The same holds true for economic analyses, however pertinent. The reinvention of China's contemporary cultural identity will play a determining role in how China approaches its future, which will have effects that determine futures beyond China. Like no time in China's recent history (and certainly unlike any time in the history of the People's Republic), China is being shaped in terms of its past: but which past (or combination of pasts) is being held up as the model—Communism, Confucianism, or Legalism? And what role are religious traditions, Buddhism, and Daoism (Taoism) playing in these models? In the pages that follow, I look at current engagements with models of China's past intending to explore the parameters and possibilities shaping China's future. I introduce traditional lenses of Chinese thought—Confucianism, Legalism, Daoism, and Buddhism—and reflect on their potential relevance for contemporary China. In short, the book is structured around two aims: to identify key aspects of China's traditions and traditional cultures and to look at ways in which these aspects are contributing to contemporary debates in China over future directions.

China and a New World Order?

There is much at stake in the new emerging dispensation. A new order that includes China (or that China leads) will contend with current issues facing our planet and the people inhabiting it. How can the nations of the world share the Earth justly, sustainably, and peacefully? Will a new order address the problems of wealth distribution, inequality, gender, and biases based on ethnicity and race? Will it propose a new order to address the growing militarization and risks of nuclear war, to promote an era of justice, sustainability, and peace? China's rise does not occur in a vacuum but alongside a number of other inquiries and discourses in the West, in the Islamic world, in the countries of the former Soviet Union and Eastern bloc, in Africa, and in Latin America. Each region of the world is going through some kind of radical reevaluation of its normative cultural traditions and aspirations, thrust between "traditional" imaginings (e.g., How Christian is Europe? How Christian should it be? How Hindu is India? How Hindu should it be? What kind of Christianity is driving American exceptionalism? What are the democratic potentialities in modern Islam? How do the countries of Southeast Asia, given their colonial and Marxist experiences, reimagine themselves in neo-traditional terms?) and modern secular aspirations. How will resident world cultures work with or oppose China's rise? How might they influence it?

No region of the world is more crucial for understanding how this new world order might take shape than Asia and, especially, China. As my chapters attempt to make clear, much is happening within China, with the much-publicized "Confucian revival," its ambiguous relationship to Marxism, the persistence of Daoism and its environmental message, and the reinvigoration of Buddhism. China also continues to deal with internal strife, ongoing human rights and "democratic" protest movements, and the repression of Islam in Xinjiang and Buddhism in Tibet. Few of these developments are visible to or understood by the rest of the world, including the West. It is especially difficult to penetrate what is happening with authentic agency within these ancient and modern cultural streams and what is being manipulated by the government for particular political or economic ends.

The task of this book is to penetrate the veil that is China and try to reveal within necessary limits what kinds of cultural retrieval, reformation, reinvention are happening. It is impossible to predict China's future or the role and consequences that its cultural retrieval, reformation, and reinvention has in influencing the policies China will take. It is likewise impossible to know what effect these will have on the international order. What we do know is the repository from which China will draw. This repository is itself vast and complex, with many dimensions both apparent and obscure. In the current world where China is playing an important role and is poised to play an even more important one in the future, it behooves us to become familiar with this repository so that we can follow forces as they unfold and even potentially exert pressure to influence their outcomes.

The "China Threat" in Contemporary Discourse

There have been several works in recent years dedicated to China, as a result of China's rise. Many of these are confrontational in tone, aimed at making us aware of, diffusing, or remedying the "China threat." These revolve around contemporary political, military or economic dynamics and assume that the current world order (or some version thereof) is the only plausible normative one. A review of these helps to position the current book within this discourse.

William J. Holstein's *The New Art of War: China's Deep Strategy Inside the United States* (2019) poses the question: how can America's fractured democracy and diverse society respond to a centrally orchestrated strategy from China that ultimately may challenge our interests and our values? This book is largely about technology transfer and the alleged theft of American technology based on the experiences of "embedded" Chinese and Chinese Americans at American companies. It also discusses how China attempts to manipulate American opinion and decision-making, all in the service of a slogan by Sun Tzu in *The Art of War*, "The supreme art of war is to subdue the enemy without fighting."

A more pessimistically framed challenge is Graham Allison's well-received book, *Destined for War: Can America and China Escape Thucydides's Trap?* (2018), which contends that China and the United States are heading toward a war neither wants. The reason is Thucydides's Trap: when a rising power threatens to displace a ruling one, violence is the likeliest result. Today, as an unstoppable China approaches an immovable America, and both Xi Jinping and former US president Donald Trump promise to make their countries "great again," make the prospects of avoiding the trap, according to Allison, grim.

Michael Pillsbury, in *Hundred-Year Marathon: China's Secret Strategy to Replace America as the Global Superpower* (2016), suggests that after forty years under American tutelage to help China build a booming economy, develop its scientific and military capabilities, and take its place on the world stage, the "China Dream" is to replace us, just as America replaced the British Empire. Based on his contacts with the "hawks" in China's military and intelligence agencies and his translations of their documents, speeches, and books, Pillsbury shows how the teachings of traditional Chinese statecraft underpin their actions. He offers an inside look at how the Chinese view America and its leaders—as barbarians who will be the architects of their own demise. *The Hundred-Year Marathon* bills itself as a wake-up call as we face the greatest national security challenge of the twenty-first century.

Two works by Peter Navarro, one coauthored with Greg Autry, *Death by China: Confronting the Dragon—A Global Call to Action* (2011), and the other with a foreword by Gordon C. Chang, *Crouching Tiger: What China's Militarism Means for the World* (2015), give a "catalogue China's abuses," "a call to action and a survival guide for a critical juncture in America's history—and the world's," and an "assessment of the probability of conflict between the United States and the rising Asian superpower." According to Chang, Navarro's *Crouching Tiger* is the ultimate "geopolitical detective story" on how China is posing the greatest challenge to the United States and to the international order. Chang's *The Coming Collapse of China* (2001) represents another aspect of the modern dialogue concerning China, that of an impending and inevitable demise resulting from deterioration from within.

Finally, there is *Bully of Asia: Why China's Dream is the New Threat to World Order* (2017) by Steven Mosher, with a byline "The Once and Future Hegemon." Mosher believes that China is an enemy that "poses a truly mortal challenge to the United States and the peaceful and prosperous world that America guarantees." He draws on China's totalitarian past (i.e., Legalism) to expose the underbelly of a Chinese "dream" intent on world domination. While Mosher's book correctly identifies Legalism, which I discuss in chapter 3, "Chinese Authoritarianism," as the historical force behind China's aggressive policies both domestic and international, it is not the only force animating China's current quest for cultural identity, as this book shows.

Another work, less confrontational in tone and more circumspect in its treatment of China, is Martin Jacques's *When China Rules the World: The End of the Western World and the Birth of a New Global Order* (2012). Jacques accepts China's rise as a given and challenges the inevitable "western drift" in orientation. In some ways, Jacques anticipates many of the assumptions of my work, particularly in suggesting that China's impact will be as much political and cultural as economic. In this regard it is complimentary, accepting China's cultural impact in a nonconfrontational tone, but is less reflective about the inherent nature of the traditions forging China's current identity.

Finally, Henry Kissinger, *On China* (2012), is masterful in his description of the inner workings of Chinese diplomacy, providing a historical perspective on Chinese foreign affairs. But the book lacks a cultural analysis of those traditions that are increasingly influencing its domestic discourse.

The current spate of books on contemporary China tends to be aggressively anti-Chinese, viewed through lenses of an assumed American natural dominance—political, economic, and cultural—and China's threat to that dominance. My book shares with Martin Jacques a more sanguine view of China's rise, accepting its inevitability and examining the dimensions into which China's cultural reinvention may be cast. This is not to say that China, like any other country or civilization, is immune to the darker forces that haunt it but to acknowledge that these forces do not exist in isolation and that these are not the only forces at play. My book is a primer for that greater intellectual landscape that is China's intellectual heritage, a heritage that is struggling to break into open modern consciousness. While those of us outside of China may only be observers of this process and the underlying forces shaping it, our awareness of these forces may help us see the shapes emerging in a more familiar light and even to make our preferences known, not in a conceptual language alien to Chinese tradition, but in terms and concepts that reveal sympathetic familiarity with it.

Chapter Summaries

The ensuing chapters tackle one by one the potential relevance of China's premodern traditions—Confucianism, Legalism, Daoism, and Buddhism—for China's contemporary cultural resurgence. The dialogue between these traditions and Chinese Communism's Marxist ideology is also enjoined.

Chapter 1, "The Return of the Native: The Fall and Rise of Confucius in Modern China," poses the question: how relevant are Confucius and his teachings to the contemporary world? It raises the perspectives of modern "New Confucians," Mou Zongsan, Tu Wei-ming, and the so-called Boston Confucians and their assertions of Confucian relevance and indeed need for addressing issues confronting contemporary societies, including Western societies beyond China and the East Asian cultural sphere facing mounting social discord. I introduce a now-classic work championing the relevance of Confucius for the modern world by Hebert Fingarette, *Confucius: The Secular as Sacred*, dating from 1972. This backdrop exposes how Confucius was denigrated and disposed of in China, yet his legacy continued to be celebrated in the Chinese diaspora community and by academics in the West. The remainder of the chapter looks into the turmoil surrounding Confucius in modern China, dating before but continuing through the Communist era. As the symbol of China's traditional culture, there is nothing so poignant as the reappearance of Confucius and his teaching in public discourse.

Chapter 2, "Chinese Authoritarianism: The Role of Legalism and Militarism in the Making of Modern China," exposes how the limitations of Confucian idealism and morality were supplemented by another deeply rooted tradition: Legalism. The Legalist tradition provides the foundations of China's bureaucratic empire and the assumption of a leading role for the use of force, including especially military force, in the exercise of power. I introduce the classic text Sunzi's *Art of War* (now well known in the West) and its contributions to Legalist thinking. I discuss in greater detail the dynastic cycle and the interplay between Confucianism and Legalism as tandem forces in the exercise of power in China. I end with a discussion about the relevance of the dynastic cycle for modern China and how Xi Jinping's promotion of Confucianism may be another instance of dressing up Legalism with a Confucian overlay.

Chapter 3, "The Daoist Cycle of Life and the Way of Returning to the Fundamental: Millenarian Prophecy and the Environmental Movement in Contemporary China," discusses the relevance of Daoism in contemporary Chinese discourse. I begin with a description of the complementary role Daoism played in the "three ways of thought in ancient China" (along with Confucianism and Legalism). I discuss the importance of the concept *dao* rooted in the classic text, the *Daode jing*: "Classic of the Way and Its Virtue/Power." I continue with a description of the relevance of Daoist concepts in contemporary Chinese debates, especially relating to the environmental movement, the so-called green Dao. I end with a different potential application of Daoist concepts for contemporary China, the "other side" of the Dao, the religious dimension of Daoism as a revolutionary force contributing to the completion of the dynastic cycle.

Chapter 4, "The Return of the Nonnative: The Buddhist Revival in Contemporary China," looks at the remarkable resurgence of Buddhism in contemporary China. In it, I examine the historical clash between Buddhism, as a foreign or nonnative religion, and a Chinese civilization constructed on Confucian morality. Beyond the historical, I look at how anti-Buddhist (and antireligious) attitudes in modern China, framed by Marxist ideology, culminated in policies aimed at suppressing and eliminating its presence. I introduce a pattern in Chinese history of suppression of Buddhism followed by revival and note the parallels with the current renaissance. Much of the chapter is dedicated to describing the modern reconstruction of two Buddhist monuments in Hangzhou, looking at them as parameters between which the contemporary revival is cast and as examples aimed at the Buddhist community of devout worshippers, on the one hand, and the phenomenal growth of leisure and tourist Buddhism, on the other. I close the chapter with reflections on the implications of the Buddhist renaissance in China for the future, especially when half of the world's Buddhists are now Chinese citizens and considering how Buddhism is situated in the context of evolving Communist Party policy toward legitimate religious expression.

Chapter 5, "Back to the Future? Prospects for Confucianism and Chinese Traditions in Contemporary China," reviews the challenges facing New Confucianism as it attempts to reformulate itself as a meaningful response to modernity. As the third iteration of Confucianism, I look at it against the backdrop of Neo-Confucianism, the second iteration of Confucianism formulated in the Song dynasty, not in terms of actual proposals, but as a template for how to respond in times of paradigmatic change. I look at two leading trends in the New Confucian movement, Mind Confucianism and Political Confucianism, to review their teachings and address their prospects, before looking at the future of China's past in terms of the support structure provided by Confucianism, Legalism, Daoism, and Buddhism for rulers in China's past and its prospects for the present and future.

I end with an afterword, "Concluding Reflections," bringing the discussion back to some of the concerns raised at the outset and the need to include China's traditions to assess the contemporary and future prospects for China and its contributions to an emerging world order.

Chapter One

The Return of the Native
The Fall and Rise of Confucius in Modern China

New Confucians and the Relevance of Confucius

Are Confucius and his teachings relevant to the contemporary world? Until recently, the response from mainland China was a resounding denial. Outside of China, in the Chinese diasporic communities and elsewhere, the reception of Confucius was more welcoming. Mou Zongsan (Mou Tsung-san; 1909–1995), a refugee from mainland China following the Communist takeover in 1949, initiated a rigorous program to reinvigorate Chinese philosophy through an encounter with Western (especially German) thought.[1] Among his prodigious achievements across a spectrum of topics in Chinese philosophy (including, especially, an interest in Tiantai Buddhism), Mou was identified as a leader in what came to be identified as the "New Confucian" (*dangdai xin rujia*) movement. In spite of the weakness that China exhibited, Mou believed that Chinese intellectual history possessed moral strengths that surpassed the West, namely "inner sagehood" (*neisheng*) and "outer kingship" (*waiwang*). "Inner sagehood" referred to a Confucian ideal of moral cultivation that Mou believed was unparalleled in the world. "Outer kingship" depicted the application of inner virtue to political governance, including the development of a productive economy and scientific and technological knowledge. The "inner sagehood/outer kingship" (*neisheng/waiwang*) distinction may be interpreted as Mou's application of the essence/function (*ti/yong*) matrix introduced in the previous chapter, which differentiates reality in terms of two aspects: an absolute aspect, the fundamental cause of origin, and a relative aspect, the concrete manifestation of the essence. Mou, likewise, asserts the moral superiority of China's essential cultural identity in the face of China's economic, scientific, and technological weaknesses. The reform of China's moral essence is unnecessary according to this line of thinking, but a strategy is needed to acquire the tools for improving China's ability to execute effective governance and for the development of a productive economy and scientific and technological knowledge.

While Mou's discussion has had a great impact on the Chinese-speaking world, his influence outside it has largely been felt through his students, particularly Tu Wei-ming (Wei-ming Tu). Tu, currently affiliated with Peking University, for many years held a professorship at Harvard University, where he became a prominent leader in a group that included both John Berthrong and Robert Neville of Boston University. Together, they and their associates formed a group known as the "Boston Confucians." The school of Boston Confucianism is well known in Chinese academic circles, where they are viewed as an indication of Confucianism's ability to be internationally relevant, to reach beyond the confines of the Chinese-speaking world. Consequently, even though their numbers are small, Boston Confucians hold great symbolic value. Their existence suggests that Confucianism can be successfully adapted to a Western perspective, that it is a tradition with rich spiritual and cultural resources that has much to teach the other world traditions. A short essay by Tu Wei-ming, "The Meaning of Life: The Big Picture," may serve as a Boston Confucian manifesto.

> Copernicus decentered the earth, Darwin relativized the god-like image of man, Marx exploded the ideology of social harmony, and Freud complicated our conscious life. They have redefined humanity for the modern age. Yet they have also empowered us, with a communal, critical self-awareness, to renew our faith in the ancient Confucian wisdom that the globe is the center of our universe and the only home for us, and that we are the guardians of the good earth, the trustees of the mandate of Heaven that enjoins us to make our bodies healthy, our hearts sensitive, our minds alert, our souls refined and our spirits brilliant [. . .] We are here because embedded in our human nature is the secret code for heaven's self-realization. Heaven is certainly omnipresent,

may even be omniscient, but is most likely not omnipotent. It needs our active participation to realize its own truth. We are heaven's partners, indeed co-creators. We serve heaven with common sense, the lack of which nowadays has brought us to the brink of self-destruction. Since we help heaven to realize itself through our self-discovery and self-understanding in day-to-day living, the ultimate meaning of life is found in our ordinary human existence.[2]

What of Boston Confucians today? In late September 2018, I attended a conference, "Rectifying the Name of Confucius," organized by the Boston University Confucian Association, held at Boston University, and sponsored by the International Confucian Association and the Confucius Institute at the University of Massachusetts–Boston (see figure 1.1 on next page). The schedule included a number of talks and panels on "Ruist Philosophy and American Life" (note: "Ru" is the Chinese pronunciation for the group that generally goes by the English name "Confucian"), "Ruist Religiosity," "Ruism in Conversation with Western Thought," and "Ruism's Historical Interaction with the West."[3] The panel sessions were punctuated with a ritual veneration ceremony on the anniversary of the 2569th year of Confucius's birth, presided over by an elderly Robert Neville and his apparent successor, a young scholar by the name of Bin Song. The ceremony was marked by an incense offering ceremony before a likeness of Confucius. Most of the forty or so attendees participated in the ceremony. In 2014, a new generation of scholars at Boston University, led by Bin Song, established the "Boston University Confucian Association," with weekly lectures and other activities open to students and the public. They formed a Facebook group, "Friends from Afar: A Confucianism Group." In addition, Bin Song has published a range of articles in the Huffington Post about Boston Confucianism. Like their predecessors, their numbers are small, but they hold the potential for Confucianism to be internationally relevant to the English-speaking world.

The initiatives of the Boston Confucians to redeem the relevance of Confucius in the English-speaking world as a tradition with rich spiritual and cultural resources that has much to teach other traditions were anticipated by Herbert Fingarette's groundbreaking little book, *Confucius: The Secular as Sacred*, originally published in 1972.[4] Remarkably, the book was issued around the same time that Cultural Revolution fervor was

20 | The Future of China's Past

Figure 1.1. Venerating Confucius at Boston University, September 30, 2018, 2,569th anniversary of Confucius's birth. Photo by author.

raging in China and at the height of the vilification of Confucius and everything he represented. Against this backdrop in mainland China, Fingarette had what can only be described as a "Come to Confucius" moment. Like others, Fingarette initially approached Confucius as a "prosaic and parochial moralizer," and his teachings contained in the *Analects* "an archaic irrelevance." Later, his view of Confucius was transformed, and he began to see Confucius as "a thinker with profound insight" who could be "a teacher to us today." His aim in the book was to "discover that which is distinctive in Confucius, to learn what he can teach me."[5]

Before delving into Fingarette's retrieval of Confucius, let me explain briefly who Confucius was. Like many important cultural icons (Moses, Jesus, Socrates, Laozi, etc.), Confucius was an obscure figure. He wrote nothing, but his teachings allegedly were recorded by students and eventually collected in a small book known as the *Lunyu*, or *Analects*. His role as a teacher and his ideas on the role of the properly trained gentleman were instrumental in forming the fundamental values that defined Chinese civilization: humaneness, ritual propriety, righteousness, reciprocity, trustworthiness, filial piety, learning, and so on. According to Confucius, and a view subscribed to by the Confucian tradition, Confucius did not initiate these values himself but served as a transmitter of them from the sage-kings of Chinese antiquity—especially Emperors Yao, Shun, and Yu—who first developed them. In reality, the sage-kings were expressions of the political ideals of later political philosophers who retroactively ascribed historical achievements to them. This created the "golden age of antiquity" as a model revered by Confucian thinkers throughout Chinese history, who invoked an ideal past as a remedy to the problems of the present.

The fundamental values mentioned above—humaneness, ritual propriety, righteousness, reciprocity, trustworthiness, filial piety, and learning—are recurring themes in the *Lunyu*. Two of these are especially prominent in the *Lunyu* and form the pillars around which Confucian philosophy unfolded. Humaneness, or *ren*, is the penultimate value of the *junzi*, the model Confucian cultured person who epitomizes moral virtue. It is characterized by the application of compassion and benevolence in the conduct of human affairs. The Sinograph for *ren* 仁 formed by depicting an upright two-legged figure 人, a human being, with the number two 二, indicating that the virtue of humaneness is the product of human interaction between people, that Confucian altruism is expressed through social interaction. Ritual propriety, or *li*, represents the Confucian idea governing the spectrum of human behaviors. The Sinograph for *li* 禮 depicts showing or revealing 示, with a ritual vessel 豊, together constituting the attitude of reverence when offering ritual sacrifices to gods or ancestors. The notion in Confucianism is expanded beyond the religious realm to include all human interactions. Righteousness, or *yi*, is added as an affirmation of correct behavior. Taken together, these three interrelated terms deal with the human agency at the heart of Confucian social interaction. *Li* is the action that has been deemed appropriate by society, the social norm if you will; *yi* is the action that is affirmed as correct according to those norms; *ren* deals with the relationship between the agent and object of the action. Reciprocity, trustworthiness, and filial piety relate to different aspects of this relationship. Learning is how one becomes aware of correct norms and how one puts them into practice correctly and appropriately through repetition until they become "natural." These fundamental values formed the basis of Confucian civilization.

As Chinese civilization spread beyond China, Confucianism had a similarly profound impact in other regions of East Asia—Korea, Japan, Vietnam—and in areas in Southeast Asia influenced by the Chinese diaspora. Premodern East Asia, especially in the last millennium, may correctly be identified as a Confucian sphere.

The problems with previous readings of Confucius and translations of the *Analects*, according to Fingarette, were multiple but reducible to two tendencies. On the one hand, it was read with Christian biases "by men instinctively and still unself-consciously bound by thinking in Christian terms, in European terms." It was admired when it affirmed Christian teachings but criticized for not reaching the higher truths of Christian revelation. This is reminiscent of Jesuit encounters with Confucianism in the sixteenth and seventeenth centuries. Jesuit missionaries, sent to China to convert heathen Chinese, were impressed by the moral character of China's Confucian culture. Alternately, they were appalled to find such morality in a faithless people, who had no concept of a Christian god, without which morality was thought by European Christians at the time to be impossible. Their reports back to Europe inspired Enlightenment thinkers like Voltaire, who famously placed a statue of Confucius in his study. Confucius would eventually become a kind of "patron saint" of the European Enlightenment.[6] The second problematic tendency for understanding the *Analects*, according to Fingarette, stemmed from either post- or non-Christian readings. In either case, interpretations of the *Analects* were colored by biases based on subjective-psychologistic readings that focused on the individual mind and the inner life and reality of the individual. In a broad sense, Fingarette is criticizing here what came to be known as the Neo-Confucian interpretation of Confucius and his teachings, the dominant Confucian tradition throughout China and East Asia during the last millennium. Neo-Confucian interpretations were a reaction against Buddhism, especially its emphasis on introspection, a key component of the meditation regimen that the various schools of Buddhist thought and practice subscribed to.

Very briefly, the history of Confucianism prior to the modern period is divisible into two developments: Classical Confucianism initiated by Confucius (551–479 BCE) and elevated to state ideology by Emperor Wu (r. 141–87 BCE) of the Han dynasty (206 BCE–220 CE); and the Confucian revival known as Neo-Confucianism initiated in the Song dynasty (960–1279), which became the basis for establishing Neo-Confucian orthodoxy in the Yuan (1279–1368), Ming (1368–1644), and Qing (1644–1912) dynasties. Between these two developments is a long interlude of Buddhist dominance, commencing after the fall of the Han dynasty, during the Three Kingdoms (220–280), Jin dynasty (266–420), Northern and Southern dynasties (420–589), and culminating in the Sui (581–618) and Tang (618–907) dynasties. Among the many aspects that Buddhism added to Chinese culture was an interiorization of the inner life of personal development through spiritual pursuits. In addition to devotional exercises, Buddhism encouraged mental cultivation through meditational practices aimed at freeing the mind of entanglements that inhibited spiritual progress. As Confucianism reinvented itself in the Song dynasty after centuries of Buddhist dominance, it inevitably adopted new aspects to make it relevant to those who had been nurtured under Buddhism. Chief among these were topics addressing Confucian approaches to metaphysical and psychological questions ranging from the nature of the mind and its relationship to fundamental principles of the universe to the role of "quiet sitting" in attaining self-realization, topics on which Classical Confucianism had had little to say. It is far too simple to reduce Neo-Confucianism to an imitation of Buddhism, but at the same time it is impossible to imagine it without influences from the Buddhist interlude that preceded it.[7]

Fingarette proposes providing a correct reading to recover the authentic Confucius as revealed in the original text of the *Analects*, one that is allegedly free of inherent biases: "a text that has unity in terms of historical-social context, linguistic style and philosophical content." There are problems with Fingarette's "unbiased" reading, and this is true of similar assertions by New Confucians. Ironically, the preoccupation with an "original" Confucius as based on a Neo-Confucian tendency. The original canon of Classical Confucianism comprised five works, allegedly edited by Confucius but not written in his own words: Classic of History, Classic of Odes/Poetry, Classic of Rites, Classic of Changes, and the Spring and Autumn Annals, especially the Zuo Commentary.

The Neo-Confucian canon, in contrast, is much reduced in size and comprises four books: Analects of Confucius, Mencius, and two short essays from the Classic of Rites, Great Learning and Doctrine of the Mean. A return to original Confucianism would not be a retrieval of Confucius's words in the *Analects* but a return to the primacy of the Five Classics, the works that were believed to be edited by Confucius himself.

In retrieving Confucius to relevancy in international intellectual circles, Fingarette predated attempts in mainland China by a couple of decades and anticipated international efforts, such as those by so-called Boston Confucians. In challenging existing interpretations of Confucius, Fingarette inadvertently raised the issue of Neo-Confucian relevancy, the mainstream of Confucian interpretation over the last millennium, to contemporary New Confucian discourse. The parameters for a New Confucianism are thus established between a Confucian fundamentalism hostile to the Neo-Confucian interpretations that preceded it, which promotes Confucian exclusivism and exceptionalism and that emphasizes an allegedly unchanging essence of Confucian teaching, and a liberal Confucianism that is inclusive and engaging and that addresses modern issues of gender and individualism from a Confucian perspective. These are themes that will be returned to in a discussion of New Confucian teachings in a later chapter.

Confucius in Tiananmen: The Return of the Native

The vilification of Confucius in China did not originate with Mao or the CCP. In many ways, the Communist Party in China was a culmination of the turn against Confucianism, not its agent. The revolt against Confucianism became forceful with the advent of the New Culture movement of the mid-1910s and 1920s, which originated in the disillusionment with traditional Chinese culture following the failure of the Chinese Republic (founded in 1912) to address China's problems. The movement began as an intellectual response to the Twenty-One Demands made by Japan in 1915 that proposed to expand Japanese control over Manchuria and the Chinese economy. The Twenty-One Demands precipitated a nationwide boycott of Japanese goods and ignited raging anger, calls to radically reform China, and for a complete introduction of Western thought and ideas to transform the literary and intellectual personality of China. Movement leaders who had studied in the West (and

Japan) called for a critical reevaluation of Chinese culture and heritage, with the Confucian system seen as the primary obstacle to reforms.

The New Culture movement called for a wholesale cultural revolution, a replacing of China's traditional culture with a new one based on Western standards, especially democracy and science. It called for an end to Confucian patriarchy in favor of individual freedom and women's liberation. Proponents, dismayed at China's weakness in international confrontations, attempted to radically change the essential basis of society in order to successfully modernize China. The focus was on introducing Western thought by destroying cultural traditions and Confucianism. In a profound sense, the New Culture movement represents the most drastic social and intellectual change ever proposed in modern Chinese history.

The New Culture movement represents a proposal unprecedented in terms of the essence/function matrix discussed previously. In all other proposals aimed at reforming China, the essence of Chinese culture—its internal moral spirit and cultural integrity—is assumed to be the root of China's strengths. The outward aspects of Chinese culture manifest functional weaknesses in terms of economic performance and scientific and technological achievements, and these are the targets of reform, not the core internal character of the Chinese spirit, which is deemed to be unsurpassable. The New Culture movement turns the assumption of the essence/function matrix on its head, proposing that *China's weakness is not functional but essential*. The way to cure China's malaise is to reform the core spirit, the essence of Chinese culture itself. This is the radical mission at the heart of the New Culture movement.

Historians like C. Y. Hsü view the New Culture movement as the third stage of China's response to the Western impact.[8] Stage 1 was represented by the "Self-Strengthening" movement (1861–1895), and proved ineffective and limited to diplomatic and military modernization but did not address the larger problems facing politics, society, and the economy. Stage 2 was presented as "Reform and Revolution" (1898–1912), with the acceptance of Western political and educational institutions, culminating in the formation of the Republic of China. Stage 3 he termed "Intellectual Awakening" (1917–1923), a further shift away from traditional Chinese modes toward complete Westernization, specifically as called for by the New Culture movement.

A significant turning point occurred within the New Culture movement with the Paris Peace Conference (a.k.a. Treaty of Versailles) following the end of the First World War. Precipitated by an announcement ceding German rights over Shandong Province to Imperial Japan on May 4, 1919, students in Beijing mounted vigorous strikes and demonstrations, turning the cultural movement into a political one that came to be known as the May Fourth movement. The inspirations that developed out of the May Fourth movement continued into the 1920s, as students, activists, and new intellectual leaders promoted a campaign against imperialism and advocated a massive modernization drive to build a new China through intellectual, literary, cultural and social reforms.

The experiences of the May Fourth movement led to reappraisals and divisions in the New Culture movement. Following the Paris Peace Conference, faith in the West was shattered. Some intellectuals began to look to more radical models of development like Marxism, Bolshevism, and anarchism. Some sought a return to Chinese traditions, while others remained faithful to Western liberal ideas as the best model for reforms. All in all, the May Fourth experience led to a division in the movement and debate over which path of Western development China should follow. Some, like Hu Shi, preferred liberalism and gradual reforms, while others, like Chen Duxiu, advocated Marxism and revolutionary change. In either case, the solution to China's social, economic, and political ills was sought in a radical departure from China's traditional essence. This essence was to be extracted and replaced with a new one of Western origin. The only question remaining was whether it would be modeled on liberal democracy or Marxist socialism, both products of European Enlightenment thought, however different in inspiration and application.

The CCP that grew out of the New Culture and May Fourth movements had two founding groups, one within China and one outside. The CCP was first founded in Shanghai in July 1921 and included among its members Chen Duxiu and Mao Zedong, who later took control of the group. The Young Communist Party (YCP) was founded in Paris in June 1922 and included prominent members Zhou Enlai and Deng Xiaoping. The different orientations of group leaders had a determinative effect over directions the party would take. Mao developed ideas about rural-based revolution in contrast to the urban-based approach of Marx and the Soviets, giving peasantry a prominent role instead of industrial workers: this became a definitive feature of early Chinese Communism's "socialism with Chinese characteristics," a euphemism for China's indigenous approach. Deng developed a pragmatic wing aiming toward a "socialism with Chinese characteristics" in which market mechanisms are given a prominent role in economic development. These two approaches were determinative for Chinese Communism.

The first thirty years of CCP rule in China, until Mao's death in 1976, were dominated by the first approach, emphasizing the Chinese peasantry as the vanguard against regressive forces in Chinese societies. Under Mao, the CCP advocated collective or governmental ownership and central government administration of the means of production and distribution of goods in the name of the people. Rule during this period was punctuated by several repressive campaigns to rid China of lingering antisocialist tendencies culminating in the Great Proletarian Cultural Revolution (1969–1976).

Important to Mao's transformation of Marxism in the Chinese context was his view of the role Confucianism played in developing a class-based feudalist society. Marx's theory of the stages of history involved an evolution of society based on organizational structures determined by primary modes of production and divisions of labor, from tribal society, primitive Communism, slave society, feudalism, capitalism, and socialism, culminating in Communism.[9] In Mao's interpretation, the major turning point from primitive Communism to a class-based feudal society in the Chinese context was marked by the development of Confucianism, and it is the Confucian element of Chinese society that persists throughout all later stages. As a result, in the Mao era, Confucianism was considered backward, counter-revolutionary, reactionary, and the repository of superstitious beliefs. It was linked with feudalism and condemned as a source of evil that plagued traditional China and whose residual influences persist to contaminate contemporary China. During the Cultural Revolution, which aimed in part to tear down what remained of the Chinese "feudal" culture, Mao vehemently denounced the Confucian belief system. The *Analects* was banned, and Confucian scholars were tortured. Red Guards overran Confucian temples, defacing statues of the sage. Confucius was branded a class enemy in a "Criticize Confucius" campaign, which championed slogans like: "Criticize the old world and build a new world with Mao Zedong Thought as a weapon," and "All erroneous ideas, all poisonous weeds, all ghosts and monsters, must be subjected to criticism; in no circumstance should they be allowed to spread unchecked." Mao's campaign was specifically directed at the "Four Olds": old customs, old culture, old habits, and old ideas. Confucius was seen as the primary perpetrator of the Four Olds and the residual elements of feudal culture. When contemporary traitors like Lin Biao, a former war hero and leading figure in mounting and promoting the Cultural Revolution, were renounced and criticized after falling out of favor with Mao, they were linked to the villainy of Confucius ("Fight well the people's battle of criticizing Lin Biao and Confucius"). The clear message was that of all the enemies of Communism in the Chinese context, none were worse than Confucius.

With the death of Mao and the persecution of the Gang of Four for their complicity in the Cultural Revolution, a new era began. Hua Guofeng was designated as successor to Mao, but he was soon eclipsed by the ascendancy of Deng Xiaoping. As paramount leader, Deng generally rejected titles but remained in firm control of party policy after his retirement in 1989 until his death in 1997. Deng instituted a pragmatic approach to governing characterized by greater tolerance, including market-based economic reforms but also a relaxation of restrictive policies on religious and intellectual expression. Third- and fourth-generation leaders Jiang Zemin (1992–2002) and Hu Jintao (2002–2012) followed Deng Xiaoping's pragmatic policies, and China experienced a "liberal moment" in its development. Leadership transitions were based on term limits, and this generation of leaders born during the Second World War represented a new technocratic style of governance and a less centralized political structure. To outside observers, China seemed to be easing its way toward a liberal democratic model.

During the period of Deng's ascendancy and the expansion of market reforms and intellectual openness, China began to show increasing signs of liberalism and tolerance. In 2008, Charter 08, a manifesto calling for government reform, involved nineteen changes, including an independent legal system, freedom of association, and the elimination of one-party rule. It faulted China as the only major world power to retain an authoritarian system that infringes on human rights.[10] The Charter 08 manifesto did not have the effect that the authors hoped for, and many, like Liu Xiaobo, who was awarded the Nobel Peace Prize in 2010, were sentenced to imprisonment for "inciting subversion of state power" as a result of their involvement. Still, Charter 08 was widely acknowledged and captured much attention. As a product of the period of openness in the early 2000s, it may be seen as an attempt to resuscitate the liberal democratic ideals and impulses of the New Culture movement that aimed to thoroughly transform China's essence not on the model of a repressive socialism but on the alternate model of reform that liberal democracy offered.[11]

At the same time, this period of relative openness inspired a massive revival and revitalization of China's intellectual and religious traditions that had long suffered under the repressive policies of the Mao era. Temples, churches, mosques, and shrines that had been either destroyed, closed, or repurposed for "productive" functions, were rebuilt and thrust back into active service once again. The impact of this revitalization will be reviewed in subsequent chapters, but in the current context, the rehabilitation of Confucius and the revival of Confucianism are of concern. As statues of Chairman Mao began to disappear from public places in China, most notably at the entrances of universities, statues of Confucius began to appear. A February 7, 1989 article in the *New York Times* called attention to Mao's declining legacy, including the removal of Mao statues at Chinese universities.[12] During roughly the same time frame, Confucius statues were being erected, most notably at resurrected and refurbished Confucian temples throughout China but also outside Chinese university libraries.

On January 14, 2011, Confucius made an unexpected return to Tiananmen Square outside the newly reopened National Museum of China, where a thirty-one-foot (9.5-meter) bronze statue of the sage was erected (see figure 1.2 on next page). A little over two months later, on April 21, the statue disappeared. Some reports indicated the removal was a result of an online uproar regarding its location, with some joking that Confucius had been banished for lacking a Beijing residency permit. The website maoflag.net, a popular forum for old-school fans of the Communist Party, celebrated the removal, with a member identified as Jiangxi Li Jianjun commenting, "The statue of the slave-owning sorcerer Confucius has been driven from Tiananmen Square!"[13] In spite of the criticisms of Mao and the rehabilitation of Confucius in China, Confucius's role in contemporary China still invites animosity.

Tiananmen is a massive square that lies at the heart of Beijing and is the site of many of China's most memorable monuments and institutions: Forbidden City, Great Hall of the People, Monument to the People's Heroes, National Museum of China, and Mao's Mausoleum. It is the fulcrum of power for the CCP and has served as the center of power in China since the Yuan dynasty (13th century). Mao Zedong, as the founder of the People's Republic of China, holds a place of privilege

30 | The Future of China's Past

Figure 1.2. A bronze statue of Confucius is pictured in front of the National Museum of China on Tiananmen Square in Beijing, China, January 11, 2011. Imaginechina Limited / Alamy Stock Photo.

in the square. His portrait graces the entrance to the Forbidden City, symbolically suggesting the presence of a new "emperor" situated at the site of the residence of the old emperors. Prior to the CCP takeover and assumption of power in 1949, an image of Chiang Kai-shek occupied the place where Mao's picture now hangs.[14] In earlier iterations of pictures at the entrance to the Forbidden City, Mao's portrait was flanked by Communist heroes: Marx, Engels, Lenin, and Stalin. This arrangement remained until the mid-1980s when I first had an opportunity to visit the square. Mao's preserved body still lies in state at the center of the square, where tourists, pilgrims, and onlookers are allowed to pass through for brief viewings under tight security. Other monuments, like that to the People's Heroes, also recall the square's Communist associations. The National Museum, outside of which Confucius's statue appeared, is dedicated to telling the story of the history of China from the perspective of the CCP's ascendance. Under these circumstances, recalling the association of the square with its revolutionary inspirations, it is not hard to imagine how the appearance of the arch-villain Confucius would incite animosity. The collision between competing antipathies—toward Confucius on the one hand and Mao on the other—may be seen as inevitable. As a retired senior Chinese official confided to me over dinner in December 2011 in Qufu, Confucius's hometown, "Not everything Mao did was praiseworthy and he caused a lot of harm, but he still accomplished a lot. We now say that 60% of what he did was good, 40% harmful, but I won't be surprised if it goes to 50/50."[15] Those who live in countries where decisions are adjudicated through popular vote will know instinctively what such lack of consensus may bode for factional infighting.

Apparently, Confucius was not deemed worthy of occupying "the nation's most hallowed slice of real estate," as it was reported in the *New York Times*.[16] If not on the square itself, where should the statue of Confucius properly be installed? A short while later, the statue of Confucius was placed in the National Museum courtyard, where it remains today. The record of Confucius's presence in the public square is a remarkable testament to where contemporary China finds itself—caught in the intersection of two worlds and two visions. Confucius's return dramatically poses the question: where does Confucius fit in the narrative of contemporary China? This question may be seen in the larger context of former Soviet republics and other modern nations that were devoted to Communism, who built large public squares to showcase the virtues of their revolutionary experience. Those nations who subsequently cast aside their revolutionary past in favor of more progressive governments have been challenged to repurpose their squares in accordance with newer national agendas.[17] In Tiananmen, Mao remains the central fixture for the time being, with Confucius relegated to a more private setting. Yet, given China's recent past, dating from the New Culture movement's renunciation of Confucian culture and Mao's vilification of Confucius, the fact that we are seeing a return of Confucius at all in China is something remarkable, as if Lazarus returned from the dead, as one of my colleagues aptly put it. I am reminded also of something Mao once famously said, according to his nephew Mao Yuanxin, "If the Communist Party has a day when it cannot rule or has met difficulty and needs to invite Confucius back, it means you (i.e., the Party) are coming to an end."[18] It remains to be seen how prophetic these words will be.

The story of Confucius's resuscitation does not end there. On September 24, 2014, President Xi Jinping delivered a surprise keynote address opening the Fifth Congress of the International Confucian Association in the Great Hall of the People (see figure 1.3).[19] As reported by Xinhua news agency, President Xi Jinping said Confucianism, founded by Confucius, has profoundly influenced Chinese civilization and has been an important part of traditional Chinese culture. "Confucianism, along with other philosophies and cultures taking shape and growing within China, are records of spiritual experiences, rational thinking and cultural achievements of the nation during its striving to build its home. . . . These cultures have nourished the flourishing Chinese nation."[20] The basic message of the address emphasized the compatibility

Figure 1.3. Xi Jinping addressing the Fifth Congress of the International Confucian Association in the Great Hall of the People, September 24, 2014. Photo by author.

between CCP values and Confucian and traditional Chinese values: that traditional Confucian values are harmonious with the values of the CCP. It also bears noting that Xi's pronouncements were not entirely new. Xi's predecessor, Hu Jintao, also stressed the need to enhance Chinese culture as the country's "soft power" in his keynote speech to the Seventeenth National Congress of the CCP in 2007.[21]

In the wake of President Xi's address, many commentated on the new direction for the CCP that Xi had outlined. The recorded statement of Wang Xuedian, executive vice-president of the Advanced Institute of Confucian Studies of Shandong University, is indicative of the public reception in China: "Chinese traditional culture, represented by Confucianism, can provide stable values to enhance social cohesion and sense of identity."[22] Nathan Gardels, editor in chief of *The World Post*, aptly headlined his article on the event (as reported in the Huffington Post): "Xi Launches Cultural Counter-Revolution To Restore Confucianism As China's Ideology."[23]

International New Confucians and China watchers also weighed in on Xi Jinping's new pro-Confucian initiative. One exchange, between Daniel Bell, a prominent New Confucian educated at McGill and Oxford, and professor of philosophy at one of China's leading universities, Tsinghua University in Beijing,[24] and Sam (a.k.a. George) Crane, professor of Political Science at Williams College, is apropos of the kinds of debates that Xi's initiative invites. Crane cites an interview given by Bell for the *New York Times*, in which Bell speaks of the positive need for Confucianism, of "a need for ethics and morals and promoting social responsibility" in an atmosphere of "increased individualism and increased sense of competition and anxiety" brought on by modern economic development. Crane's response exposes deeper fault lines:

> I see . . . a certain irony [in Bell's comment]: it is precisely when China has grown the farthest from its Confucian past, with the rise of culturally individualizing materialist competition, that some people there seek to reconnect with the tradition. In other words, China is not now a Confucian society and the Confucian revival there will not fundamentally redirect Chinese modernization. Whatever "Confucianism" arises there in the next few years and decades will likely be a shallow imitation of the original because the ethical demands of Confucius are too restrictive to modern lifestyles and behavior.

While it may be true that certain individuals will find the commitment and fortitude to enact duty according to ritual and progress toward humanity in a manner consistent with Confucius's thought, not enough individuals will do so to justify defining China as a "Confucian" society. The tension between Confucian morality and modern life is just too great.[25]

As an indication of the speed with which political winds change in Beijing, the day following President Xi's address to the Congress of the International Confucian Association, an event that was widely reported in Chinese news outlets and on Chinese television, the small bookstore of the hotel we were accommodated in made a quick adjustment to one of its collections. While the bookstore was small, I had noted previously that it had some surprisingly good volumes, one, in particular, being the *House Sayings of Confucius* (*Kongzi jiayu*), comprising four volumes of teachings attributed to the sage. As I scurried through the bookstore the following morning, I saw that they had placed the volumes out front and covered them with a makeshift handwritten banner, AS RECOMMENDED BY XI JINPING. The banner held more interest for me at that moment than the actual contents. It provided visible, concrete proof of the impact of Xi's decision to embrace Confucius and traditional Chinese culture. While many Chinese might indeed welcome the return of Confucius and China's traditional cultures, others were open to the economic incentives that a cultural renaissance based on Confucianism and China's traditional cultures might hold. It would come as no surprise that a listing in the *China Daily* dated May 12, 2017, announced a new book by Xi Jinping translated into English, *Xi Jinping: How to Read Confucius and Other Chinese Classical Thinkers*. "This new collection" it states, "lists over 200 classical quotations and reflects the achievements of Xi Jinping's extensive reading and diligent studies."[26] It also comes as no surprise that the Confucian Research Institute, in Confucius's hometown of Qufu (Shandong Province) has become a center for the dissemination of Confucian teachings and ideas.[27]

Xi Jinping's Promotion of Confucianism: Can the "Four Olds" Be Made New Again?

The remarkable resuscitation of Confucianism in contemporary China, a tradition believed to be all but dead until recently, presents an opportunity to question the dynamics at work in China itself. Sam Crane deftly indicated how things may not be as they seem and that the promotion of Confucianism may be a shield against the ravages of other forces. Among the onslaught of questions (Why Confucianism? Why now? To what end?) I can offer no conclusive statements. The nature of contemporary China is, as modern China has always been, too elusive, too subject to the vagaries of the circumstances it finds itself in, to offer definitive answers. I can only situate the debates about the directions China is aiming toward in the context they are themselves situated in.

Given the tendency of China's reform-minded culture since the New Culture and May Fourth movements, one can only find the return of Confucianism and Chinese traditional cultures a baffling about-face. But this is only true if one takes the development literally, without situating the context that precipitated it. As Xi Jinping assumed power, he identified corruption as the biggest threat to CCP's continued dominance. The aim of the CCP, as Xi Jinping and Deng Xiaoping have both asserted in their respective ways, is self-preservation, to be the sole party of political power in China. The sole heretical decision of the party would be to invite legitimate competition with itself. All mechanisms available to assure the preservation of power for the Communist Party are admissible. In spite of any lingering affection for liberal forms of government remaining from the New Culture movement, the Communist Party assumes itself as the sole authority of the nation. President Xi's affection for Confucianism is largely a function of his taste for authoritarianism. Long centuries of imperial rule provide a model for an authoritarian government that, when functioning effectively, remains unchallenged. Xi's appetite for Confucianism is wedded to the model for authoritarian rule that it sanctions.

The decline of Marxist ideology in China left a moral vacuum at the core of Chinese life. In the absence of traditional moral restraints, such as those provided by Confucianism, Marxism provided a model for proper socialist behavior devoted to a common good and free of the individualistic excesses (i.e., greed) of capitalism. Deng Xiaoping's capitalist market reforms did wonders for the Chinese economy, depressed as it was after decades of stagnation, warfare, and the suppressive forces of state-managed controls. Along with the wealth they created, these market reforms introduced unprecedented levels of corruption as Deng's "to get rich is glorious" slogan was interpreted as a rush to wealth at any cost, regardless of consequences. The socialist appetite for a common good was quickly dashed in the name of ruthless capitalist competition.

Perhaps Xi Jinping sees in Confucian distaste for merchant wealth a similar blight on society that Communists detect in unbridled capitalism, and this is a kinship he hopes to forge. At any rate, Xi sees Confucianism as an antidote to the moral vacuum left by the decline in influence of Marxist ideology and a solution to the corruption that had become rife in the CCP and Chinese society as a whole. In traditional China, social disruption inducing corruption is a leading cause of dynastic change. In imperial China, the only mechanism for political change is revolution, inspired by dissatisfaction among the people in search of social upheaval. Seen in this light, the growing dissatisfaction among regular Chinese can only be seen as a potential pretext for revolt.

The euphemistic phrase "Socialism with Chinese characteristics" heralds the possibilities for China's experimentation with socialist principles to incorporate indigenous elements. Deng Xiaoping used it as a pretext for capitalist market reforms, an otherwise stark reversal of anything Marx stood for. Xi Jinping uses it to introduce Confucian moral reforms, an equally bold move in the context of Chinese Communism and its wholesale rejection of a feudal culture associated with Confucius's name. This reversal signals a wholesale rejection of the New Culture and May Fourth movements, which sought China's social, political, and economic renewal based on a "new culture" imported from the West. This "new culture" would replace an outdated Confucian cultural system—extracting an old essence and replacing it with a new one. Does the return of Confucius suggest a return to a new "self-strengthening movement," an assertion of a core of essential indigenous values alongside an adaptation of Western science and technology? While repudiating New Culture movement aspirations, it signals a return to deeper impulses toward cultural autonomy free of outside influences. How illusory this freedom from external influence may be is, of course, open to debate, however much indigenous voices remain certain of their authenticity.

It is also important to acknowledge that while Xi Jinping's address singled out Confucianism, he also acknowledged the roles played by other aspects of traditional Chinese culture. "Confucianism, along with other philosophies and cultures," he stated, "are records of spiritual experiences, rational thinking, and cultural achievements. . . . These cultures have nourished the flourishing Chinese nation." In Xi's appraisal, the renaissance of China in the contemporary world is more than just the return of Confucianism. What role do other traditions play, and are all traditions equally valuable in this regard? Where is the line drawn that makes some aspects of the tradition valuable while others are not? Is it possible to talk of dividing different aspects or groups of religious traditions bearing the same name, some aspects legitimate and others not?

At this juncture and for the foreseeable future, we must still acknowledge the CCP rather than a Chinese Confucian Party as the primary authority in China, for it is the CCP that controls Confucianism rather than the other way around. Xi Jinping has found a way to make Confucianism (and other traditions) useful as tools in the CCP arsenal, and this has given it (and them) a seat at the table, so to speak. But it is still very much a table set by the CCP and with CCP preservation in mind. Yet, as I have attempted to point out, there is an intrinsic contradiction in the marriage between the CCP and Confucianism. This contradiction is not, as many may suppose, based on rival ideological claims. Confucianism and Communism do represent rival ideologies, to be sure, but they also have points of compatibility, as suggested above. The real nature of their contradiction has to do with their rival proposals vis-à-vis the Self-Strengthening and New Culture movements, whether Confucianism is a source of China's essential spiritual strength, unrivaled in the world, or the cause of its weakness and inability to successfully modernize. The CCP has successfully managed other contradictions, and there is no reason that it won't be able to manage this one as well; however, the nature of the marriage is such that certain fault lines and tensions are bound to be exposed, and the CCP ability to handle these will determine its ongoing success.

Of the crises facing the Party, I point out two here that are emblematic. The first involves a rising luminary and potential Party leader, Bo Xilai. Bo is the son of Bo Yibo (1908–2007), a political and military leader who was one of the most senior political figures in China during the 1980s and 1990s. The senior Bo was one of a select group of powerful veterans centered on Deng Xiaoping who became informally known as the "Eight Immortals" for their political longevity and for the vast influence they commanded. As the son of Bo Yibo, Bo Xilai was regarded as one of the Party's "Crown Princes," or "Princelings" (a description that applies to Xi Jinping as well, as son of Chinese Communist veteran Xi Zhongxun), a designation for the sons of prominent and influential senior leaders in the Communist Party. The junior Bo was seen as a rising star within the Party, considered a likely candidate for promotion to the elite Politburo Standing Committee at the Eighteenth Party Congress in 2012. Bo had made a name for himself as a promoter of the "Chongqing model" advocated by the Chinese New Left, critical of capitalism and the economic reforms initiated in the Deng era. Inflamed by growing economic inequality, Bo launched campaigns against organized crime and corruption and increased spending on social programs. Bo also initiated a nostalgic return to Cultural Revolution–era "red culture" and the era of Maoist-style socialism.

Bo Xilai's rise to prominence was suddenly halted in the wake of the Wang Lijun incident. Wang, Bo's top lieutenant and police chief, was alleged to have information involving corruption implicating Bo's role in an attempted cover-up of murdered British businessman Neil Heywood. Heywood was a close associate of Bo's wife, Gu Kailai, and the three allegedly had close financial ties. As Wang brought information about the nefarious activities to light, he sought asylum in the American consulate in Chengdu, ostensibly fearing for his life. In the aftermath, Bo was removed from his position as Party chief on Chongqing and lost his seat on the Politburo; he was later removed from all Party positions, lost his seat at the National People's Congress, and was expelled from the Party altogether. Found guilty of corruption, Bo was sentenced to life in prison.

Bo's rise and subsequent fall from grace expose fault lines in CCP governance during the Xi Jinping era. It reveals the depth of corruption and sense of entitlement within the Party, of which Bo Xilai may be regarded as the tip of the iceberg. Following Bo's trial and incarceration, a number of high-profile cases of corruption involving leading Party officials have been prosecuted. In 2015, China issued a list of its top one hundred officials and others wanted on suspicion of corruption who were believed to have fled abroad, the majority of whom were in the United States and Canada, a further sign of Xi Jinping's campaign against graft within the Party.[28] The fact that Bo's lieutenant, Wang Lijun, sought refuge in the US Consulate is extremely telling. What does it mean when top officials of a country cannot seek refuge with their own government in their own country? There can be fewer more damning condemnations than this. While Xi Jinping's campaign has been designed to root out financial corruption, what of the moral rot that the Bo Xilai incident exposes for the CCP as a whole? While Bo Xilai championed a return to Maoist era "red culture" in line with the aspirations of China's New Left, his socialist values were but a thin veneer covering his corrupt and authoritarian impulses. It is easy to understand in this context how Xi Jinping resorts to Confucianism and traditional values in an attempt to win back a measure of confidence in CCP rule in China. Can Xi maintain a Marxist posture with a Confucian moral core?

The second crisis I point to as emblematic of the challenges that the CCP faces under Xi Jinping's stewardship involves a group of young Marxists from Peking University, exemplified by Yue Xin. Yue Xin, a self-proclaimed feminist and Marxist, gained attention in April 2018 as a leading figure in China's #MeToo movement for pressing a freedom of information request involving a former Peking University professor's alleged rape of a female student and her subsequent suicide some twenty years ago. According to Yue, she faced strong pressure from university officials to rescind her request.[29] More recently, in August 2018, Yue was involved in protests by the student labor organization JASIC Workers Solidarity Group pressing for better working conditions and increased pay. The workers attempted to form a union in defiance of China's prohibition against independent unions organized outside of state sanction. The province of Guangdong, where the action took place, is known for the "Guangdong model," a relatively liberal application of economic and social policies, giving freer rein to businesses and corporations to pursue profit without restricting regulations. The model's focus on economic liberalization ignores issues with industry practices and social welfare.[30] The dispute led to the arrest of some fifty student protestors, including Yue Xin. Yue Xin has not been seen or heard from since.[31] As of December 30, 2018, her whereabouts remained unknown.[32]

What is intriguing about the episode involving Yue Xin is that it represents an example of a Chinese Marxist challenging the allegedly Marxist state in the name of Marxist socialist principles. In the recent National People's Congress held in the spring of 2018, Xi Jinping instituted a fourteen-point program of fundamental principles for socialism with Chinese characteristics.[33] In spite of (or because of) his support for Confucianism, Xi Jinping made it clear that China was a Marxist state. In his address on May Fourth to commemorate the two hundredth anniversary of the birth of Karl Marx, Xi commented:

> Today, we commemorate Marx in order to pay tribute to the greatest thinker in the history of mankind and also to declare our firm belief in the scientific truth of Marxism. . . . Writing Marxism onto the flag of the Chinese Communist Party was totally correct . . . . Unceasingly promoting the sinification and modernisation of Marxism is totally correct. . . . We must

win the advantages, win the initiative, and win the future. We must continuously improve the ability to use Marxism to analyse and solve practical problems.[34]

This may be little more than Xi Jinping the politician weighing the forces of discontent within the Party over his recent assertions of compatibility with Confucian moral values against an entrenched Marxist wing. And yet, the Marxist wing itself continues to show signs of displeasure.

On August 19, 2018, Yue Xin issued an open letter to Xi Jinping and the CCP Central Committee expressing support for the protesting JASIC workers.[35] Remarkably, she situated her support for the workers within Xi Jinping's highly publicized and constitutionally enshrined rhetoric on "socialism with Chinese Characteristics for a new era," indicating how, for China's young Marxist millennials, the CCP isn't Marxist enough.[36] Her letter challenges the CCP's interpretation of Marxism, its tolerance for the glaring inequalities in Chinese society, and its lack of support for the workers' group. To learn real Marxism, Yue contends, one must look beyond the CCP's sanctioned and mandated curriculum and read on one's own. Yue Xin's example exposes the limits of CCP tolerance for socialist-inspired critiques and the uneasy balance that Xi Jinping's CCP must strike between existing tensions.[37] The Party has been aware of this issue. Recognition of tensions exposed by economic inequality is evident in policies advocated in CCP Five-Year Plans from 2005 on, when the Party called for "Harmonious Society" (*hexie shehui*). The failure of policies to correct inequalities and ongoing gaps between rich and poor in China provides fertile ground for dissension.

The glue that holds these tensions together has less to do with Marxism or Confucianism and is more attributable to the CCP's authoritarian grasp on the mechanisms of political power. In the next chapter, I explore the important role that a less acknowledged tradition in China known as Legalism has in the successful execution of CCP rule in China, including the recent resumption of rule without term limits, or "rule for life," of Xi Jinping. As much as the future of China's past may lean on Confucianism for assistance, China's authoritarian instincts are significantly bolstered by the tenets of Legalism.

Chapter Two

Chinese Authoritarianism

The Role of Legalism and Militarism in the Making of Modern China

Why Is Confucianism Not Enough?

Andre Malraux, the famous author and statesman of France, once visited Japan and responded to a reporter's question about differences between China and Japan: "China didn't have warrior spirit. [In] the West Europe had chivalry, and India had it, too. But only China didn't have it."[1] Malraux summarized a common perception of a China traditionally ruled by an effete class that lacked warrior spirit (in other words Confucians). The ideal society according to Confucianism consisted of four classes in descending order: a relatively small Confucian educated elite, a large class of farmers/peasants who served as the mainstay of an agrarian-based economy, a class of artisans who provided the tools and implements needed for society to function, and a class of merchants who the Confucians regarded negatively as a burdensome group who managed society's wealth without actually producing anything themselves. Graphically, the structure of the ideal Confucian society may be depicted as a pyramid (see figure 2.1 on next page).

Malraux inadvertently points out what makes the ideal Confucian social structure problematic and what is missing. In fact, the Confucian ideal of four classes was rarely, if ever, realized in actual practice.[2] The low status of merchants and the absence of the military were belied by the roles played by each throughout Chinese history. Ever since Emperor

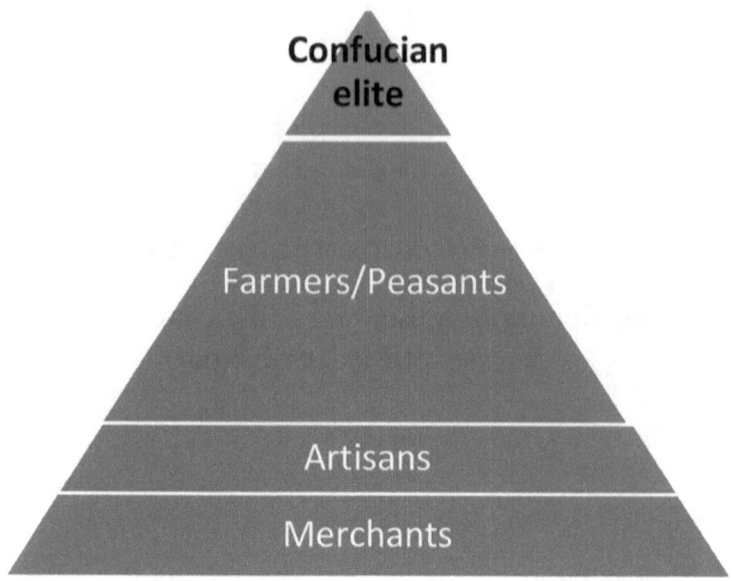

Four Classes according to Confucianism

Figure 2.1. Four Classes according to Confucianism. Author provided.

Wu (r. 14–187 BCE) of the Han dynasty (206 BCE–220 CE) promoted Confucian doctrines, relied on Confucian advisors, and established Confucian institutions, Confucianism has been hailed as the center of the Chinese tradition. The reality, however, was quite different. Emperor Wu's promotion of Confucianism did not interrupt his continuation of the system of rewards and punishments and administrative methods of his predecessor, the first great unifier of China, Shihuangdi, who reigned as king of Qin (r. 247–220 BCE) and the first emperor of the Qin dynasty (221–206 BCE). This system of administrative methods and standards goes by the name of Legalism (in Chinese, *Fajia*). In it lies the foundations of China's bureaucratic empire and the assumption of a leading role for the use of force, including especially military force, in the exercise of power.

The six arts of ancient China included the military arts of charioteering and archery, in addition to ritual performance and musical artistry, and writing skills and mathematics. These were areas that any self-respecting gentleman wished to demonstrate expertise in. This ancient ideal of gentlemanly arts practiced in concert, a kind of Chinese equivalent to a "renaissance man," eventually gave way to a more dedicated class engaged in the practice of warfare as an end in itself. The turning point is codified in the works of the famed military strategist, Sunzi, whose *Art of War* has become required reading by military (and business) strategists. Before Sunzi, war was conducted according to the gentleman's code. Winning was not the only desired outcome of military conflict but was deemed as one pursuit among many. The overriding concern was for conduct as an expression of virtue, a sort of "it doesn't matter whether one wins or loses" but how one comports oneself according to standards of gentlemanly virtue. It is in this regard that a professional military was deemed unnecessary and not in keeping with the ideals of a good Confucian society. After Sunzi, ideas about conduct in war changed. War is no longer about virtue but about winning. To ensure victory, one must take advantage of opportunities as they present themselves. The headings of the *Art of War* indicate the strategic nature of the topics addressed: (1) "Detail Assessment and Planning," (2) "Waging War," (3) "Strategic Attack," (4) "Disposition of the Army," (5) "Military Forces," (6) "Weaknesses and Strengths," (7) "Military Maneuvers," (8) "Variations and Adaptability," (9) "Movement and Development of Troops," (10) "Terrain," (11) "The Nine Battlegrounds," (12) "Attacking with Fire," and (13) "Intelligence and Espionage." For Sunzi, the military becomes an essential aspect of government strategy, not something disdained by an elite class who looked on military engagement as a sporting necessity and an arena in which to demonstrate their virtue as gentlemen. Military strategy becomes an aspect of government intelligence, where "the supreme art of war is to subdue the enemy without fighting," where "every battle is won before it is fought."

Sunzi's *Art of War* was readily incorporated into the ancient Chinese school of thought known as Legalism, introduced above. Legalism is, above all else, the exercise of power, the use of authority to increase wealth and expand territory. While the English translation would seem to indicate a preference for the "rule of law," Legalists, in fact, were experts in administrative methods, and the school represented several branches of realistic statesmen or "men of methods" in ancient China. Legalism was foundational for the traditional Chinese bureaucratic empire. Describing Legalists as "Theorists of the State," the French Sinologist

Jacques Gernet considered Legalism the most important tradition of the fourth and third centuries BCE,[3] an assessment that nearly all would agree with. The Legalists were the first to conceive of the state as an empire with a centralized bureaucracy and administration and not just a conglomeration of families and villages. They concentrated on the accumulation of wealth and power, and as a result, are often compared with Machiavelli and considered akin to realpolitik thought in a Chinese context. They ignored morality as a basis for governing, as well as questions of how a society should ideally function. They examined contemporary realities, emphasizing how best to consolidate wealth and power in the hands of an autocratic ruler and state. Their foremost goal was achieving increased order, security, and stability.

The contributions of Legalist thought include the institution of administrative measures, the concept that effective government required skilled system design, implemented by a bureaucratic chain of command through the demarcation of administrative subunits. They called for government oversight of the citizenry through the registration of households. The economy and taxation were administered by the central government with proceeds going directly to the state. Weights and measures were standardized to ease the flow of goods throughout the empire. They promulgated a law code and penal measures to ensure proper conduct according to government dictates, believing that good conduct cannot be presumed but can only be assured by coercive measures. In this, they determined, against their Confucian detractors, that the rule of law superseded rule by virtue and that the only effective means of governance is to presume an avaricious nature that can only be curbed by the threat of external punishments and prohibitions. Government was executed through a centralized, statewide administration of magistrates with allegiance directly to the ruler rather than local power holders. The state also worked to disintegrate large multilineal clans in favor of a nuclear family structure with fewer means to contravene state dictates. To ensure border security, the government staffed a large, well-equipped army that also facilitated the expansion of territory where possible. To ensure domestic security, the government staffed a large contingent of security forces that enacted brutal policies against any who contravened the goals of the state.

The Legalist turn in Chinese thinking also has links to Confucianism. In the third century BCE, one of Confucianism's greatest classical thinkers, Xunzi (often ranked after Confucius and Mencius), allowed that laws and punishments may play a legitimate role in the exercise of state power but only as supplementary tools for rulers who had demonstrated their moral virtue and only as a way to inspire people toward ethical self-improvement.[4] Xunzi's attraction to more punitive measures was a corollary to his famous pronouncement that human nature is, at base, evil and therefore in need of correcting in order to realize its full potential. In this, he stood in marked contrast to Mencius who took the opposite approach in regarding human nature as essentially good and that evil behavior is the result of adverse circumstances that force people into poor choices. As the Confucian tradition mainly sided with Mencius's view, Xunzi's theory was marginalized, and its influence may have remained so if not for it being taken up by his pupil, Li Si, who "discarded the ethical dimensions of Xunzi's teachings and retained only the Legalistically inclined pragmatic elements."[5]

The role of militarism in China is further evidenced by the so-called Seven Military Classics, a canonized group of texts including Sunzi's *Art of War*, many of which date from the Warring States period of Chinese history (ca. 475–221 BCE).[6] Notably, some of these texts include content attempting to synthesize Confucianism and Legalism. The *Wuzi*, for example, attempts to resolve Confucian humanistic concerns for benevolent government based on moral values with Legalist measures for regulating behaviors based on strict criteria (i.e., rewards and punishments).

The Dynastic Cycle: The Interplay between Confucianism and Legalism

The reality of rule in imperial China was not a simple expression of government benevolence according to Confucian principles, no matter how frequently and effectively Confucian scholars and historians evoked this ideal, but a dialectic between the arts of war and peace: The Way of Warriors (the Art of War sanctioned by Legalism) versus the Way of Benevolence (Humane Conduct sanctioned by Confucianism). In theory, the "mandate of Heaven," the Confucian enshrined principle of divine sanction for imperial rule, determined that all rulers were decided by Heaven as an acknowledgment of their superior moral virtue. In reality, a tension permeated imperial rulership in Chinese history, fluctuating between the notion of emperors as warlords versus emperors as moral exemplars following the dictates of Confucian principles. According to Confucian teaching, the warlord is never a legitimate ruler but a usurper who achieves his position not through moral example but through the exercise of authoritarian rule backed by brute force. The reality demanded that in virtually every case, a dynastic founder achieved his position through the exercise of his military power, besting rivals on the battlefield to win his role. This reality is revealed in the famous advice allegedly proffered to Kublai Khan by his minister: "Conquering the world on horseback is easy; it is dismounting and governing that is hard."[7] The advice reveals the dynamic of imperial rule in China. China is conquered by brute force but must be administered judiciously to ensure the success and longevity of the dynasty. This sets up the classic struggle in Chinese politics between the power of the word (in Chinese *wen*, indicating literature or the culture of letters) versus military might (in Chinese *wu*, military prowess).

The key to a successful dynasty is to translate military success into administrative effectiveness. Military success depends on soldiers and armaments. Administrative effectiveness relies on knowledge and the power of the pen. Dynastic founders typically start out as hegemonic rulers who acquire rule through military prowess. To be sure, the Confucian tradition, as previously mentioned, makes a significant distinction between the way of the hegemonic ruler (*ba dao*) and the way of enlightened rule by virtue (*wang dao*). Only the latter is regarded as true and authentic. In reality, the transition from *wu* to *wen*, from hegemon to enlightened ruler is a transition that must be demonstrated after the fact. How hegemonic proclivities evolve in the wake of the successful conclusion of combat is filled with uncertainty, reflecting the ruler's temperament and the circumstances surrounding the peace he has won. Have all rivals been vanquished? Has peace created new ones? What political factions are there to contend with? The questions surrounding the circumstances are as endless and varied as rulers themselves. The threat of hegemonic tendencies often animates the reality of imperial rule after the dynasty is established. Legalist authority based on force is an avenue available to all emperors and is often evoked under the guise of an otherwise "Confucian" administration. In short, however, the successful dynastic transition from *wu* to *wen* involves establishing a literary-based culture. The transition to *wen* entails empowering the bureaucracy of scholar-officials and diminishing the vital role previously played by the military.

In the Chinese context, the study of Confucianism is central to the creation of a bureaucracy of scholar-officials.

This brings us to something known as the "dynastic cycle" in imperial China, which attempts to explain the dynamics of dynastic rule and dynastic change. One of the first things that one learns about when studying imperial China is the "mandate of Heaven," mentioned above. The mandate of heaven purports to explain how imperial power is attained and preserved in dynastic history. According to this concept, heaven embodies the natural order and divine will of the universe. It grants the mandate to a virtuous ruler, referred to as the "son of Heaven." When a ruler is deposed, it is deemed an indication that the ruler lacks virtue, and as a consequence, the mandate is revoked. Natural disasters such as famines and floods, earthquakes, comments, and other aberrations of the celestial order are taken as signs of heaven's displeasure with the ruler, and a potential indication of impending dynastic change. In order to perpetuate dynastic rule, emperors had to demonstrate an ability to cultivate peace and prosperity in addition to achieving success on the battlefield.

How the dynastic cycle accounts for the change of dynasty applies a mechanism that is less than precise and open to interpretation. Every dynasty, in principle, is founded by a "great hero" who allegedly acquires heaven's favor as a result of his superior virtue. Once power is acquired, the founder immediately sets out to create the conditions for peace and prosperity in his regime. Government reforms are enacted to establish the agenda of the new regime through proactive policies. If successful, the lives of the common people improve, agriculture flourishes, and taxes are reduced. As wealth increases, however, corruption occurs. Friction with neighboring countries attracted by China's largesse, typically from the north, poses the threat of conflict. Arming and supplying the military results in an increase in taxation, not to mention the added burden from the conscription of sons into military service, diverting their much-needed labor from agriculture. Disasters from a variety of potential sources—floods, droughts, famine, invasions, revolts—inevitably occur, contributing to further disruptions to the economy and society. At this point, the mandate of the dynasty is in jeopardy, and rebellion is deemed justifiable. Groups of disgruntled peasants form around leaders who call for reform. Eventually, a strong leader emerges to unite rebel groups to challenge the emperor, and the emperor is overthrown in a violent revolution. The victorious leader declares himself a new emperor, recipient of Heaven's mandate. The history books award him a noble rank by virtue of his lofty spirit and superior virtue. He is the "great hero" of a new dynasty, and the pattern repeats itself. The dynamic dictates that all dynastic founders are virtuous heroes; emperors who preside over the end of a dynasty are depraved villains. The patterns of Chinese history are animated by the notion of Heaven's mandate and the "great hero" hypothesis, which provides a moral mechanism to explain a dynasty's rise and flourishing as well as its decline and fall. Depicted graphically, the dynastic cycle in China appears in figure 2.2.

The cycle suggests how warlords become emperors, and how the model of the emperor evolves over time. The founding emperor is a battle-hardened military commander who wins admiration through his military prowess. Once crowned emperor, he remains a hands-on decision maker, dictating commands to his administrators in much the same way he formerly executed strategy on the battlefield through his military generals. Many of the administrators, indeed, are culled from the ranks of his former generals. The real transition from military-style governing to civil administration occurs through the vastly different training and experience of the founding emperor's successors. The second emperor of a dynasty may be of an age where he personally experiences the battlefield, or at least recalls his father's direct lessons from it, but by the third emperor of a dynasty, the

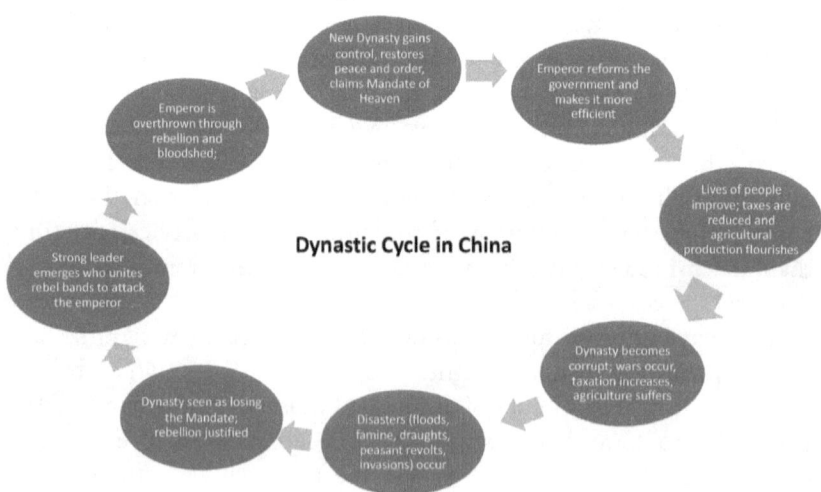

Figure 2.2. Dynastic cycle in China. Author provided.

battlefield may begin to appear as something "long ago and far away," a fading reality that has little to do with any actual functioning of the government. Emperors at this stage, if their tutors have been effective, are much more conversant in the arts of peace than the arts of war. Their Confucian teachers will have instilled in them an appreciation for *wen*, the culture of letters, over *wu*, the power of military might.

This brings us to a pattern that may be termed the "Bureaucratic Cycle," the pattern of government control and authority in imperial China that explains the transition from the "great hero," the dynastic founder, to bureaucratic control, where control of the government passes from emperor to bureaucracy. As outlined above, founding dynastic emperors were typically warlords skilled in the art of war. These emperors were autocrats with "hands-on" decision-making power. The crown prince, however, lived in a time of peace. As a protégé tutored by Confucian scholars skilled in the arts of peace, future emperors learned very different lessons. In theory, they were counseled to seek and follow the advice of their mentors, senior scholar-officials who executed the levers of power in their regime. From hands-on autocrats used to directing generals on the battlefield, the imperial position evolved into the head of the bureaucracy who seeks their advice and rules judiciously based on their counsel. This marked the ascendancy of the bureaucracy in imperial decision making and the execution of government policy. In extreme cases, the emperor became a mere puppet beholden to the bureaucracy (or other power-holding groups such as eunuchs or members of the imperial family).

Notwithstanding the realities of strong individual emperors who exercise their prerogative and seize the levers of power for themselves, thus invoking their autocratic privileges, the bureaucratic cycle in any given dynasty tended to operate in the following fashion. Dynastic founders were essentially hegemonic rulers who acquired rule through military prowess based on principles of Legalism. Successful dynastic transition moved from *wu* to *wen* as its operating principle to establish literary-based cultures. The transition to *wen* entailed empowering the bureaucracy as a class of scholar-officials expert in Confucianism. In the process, the position of the emperor evolved from "emperor as military general" to "emperor as head of bureaucracy." By design, Confucians subjugated and devalued the military, which remained unrecognized in the hypothetically ideal Confucian state.

All of this, of course, is but a gross oversimplification of the complex of forces and idiosyncratic circumstances that constitute any particular dynasty and its emperors. But it is instructive, I believe, to see the pattern implicit in this outline, to see it still at work in broad strokes in contemporary China. The period of imperial Chinese history has ended, but the forces animating Chinese history remain to haunt the present regardless of how determined Chinese modernizers have been to leave them behind. Confucianism may be the buttress for the "culture of letters" that the Chinese tradition relishes, but Legalism is the handmaiden that aids and abets the reality of gaining and maintaining power through force, without which it could not exist. The patterns of dynastic formation and decline are realized through this relationship between Legalism and Confucianism in the exercise of power.

The trends summarized here are, to a fair degree, historically attested in the major dynasties of Chinese history, the Han (202 BCE–22 CE), Tang (618–907), Song (960–1279), Ming (1368–1644), and Qing (1636–1912), all of which endured for well over two hundred years. Each followed some semblance of the pattern described here as the dynastic cycle, starting with the establishment of peace and order and a claim of a new mandate from Heaven, improved living standards with the promulgation of efficient government policies, followed by tensions resulting from corruption, civil unrest, and natural disasters. These are taken as signs that the government is losing the mandate, and new leaders emerge to contest the throne. Eventually, one of them succeeds in deposing the ruler and establishing himself as the new emperor, equipped with Heaven's mandate, to usher in a new era of peace and prosperity.

The Dynastic Cycle and Modern China

How does any of this relate to modern China and the rule of Xi Jinping? To consider how China's past is affecting the present and future, we must consider the influence of the imperial dynastic cycle to modern and contemporary China. The first question is this: is the dynastic cycle applicable? Some will argue that the disruptions involved in China's tortured transition from its imperial period to modernity are such that they render it inconsequential. Modern China operates on principles divorced from this past and the dynastic cycle, a product of the imperial period, is no longer relevant. China is no longer ruled by an emperor, Confucianism is no longer the operative thought system of modern China, and the institutional and social structures permeating Chinese culture are markedly different than those in the past. All of this is true, of course, but the past has a way of peeking through the cracks in modern China (and elsewhere) in unexpected places. Xi Jinping's recent evocation of Confucianism and the traditions of China's past are a reminder that the past continues to resonate, even so far as to receive official acknowledgment (as discussed in the previous chapter). In the context of the current chapter, I would like to revisit the authoritarian tendencies of China's past, namely China's Legalist tradition, in light of the current manifestation, the authoritarian regime of the CCP.

If we look at generational transitions in CCP leadership, it is easy to assign to Mao Zedong the role of "great hero" and "dynastic" founder. Mao epitomizes the autocratic ruler who seizes control of the empire through victory on the battlefield. Mao continued his dominance through his reign as China's supreme leader, crushing any opposition that emerged, perceived or otherwise, often in ruthless style. In this regard, Mao is comparable to China's paradigmatic autocratic emperor, Shihuangdi of the Qin dynasty, as previously introduced, who united China through a brutal assumption of power and force buttressed by Legalist philosophy. Because of Mao's attempt at a full-scale transformation of China and the complete overthrow of its past traditions, he invites comparison with Shihuangdi, who attempted a similarly massive overhaul. His full name, Qin Shihuangdi, literally translates as "First Emperor of Qin." The name of the first imperial dynasty, Qin, became associated with the tradition that Shihuangdi initiated and formed the basis for the English name "China." (In Chinese, China is known as Zhongguo, the "Middle or Central Kingdom," acknowledging its predominant role in the world, traditionally confined to the known world, primarily Asia.) Huangdi combined two titles—*huang* of the three sovereigns (*san huang*) and the *di* of the legendary Five Emperors (*wu di*) of Chinese prehistory. The title was intended to appropriate some of the prestige of Huangdi, the "Yellow Emperor," considered a founder of the Chinese people.

Shihuangdi was a ruthless ruler who followed the dictates of Legalism to amass absolute power and authority in the ruler. Because of this and his disdain for Confucianism and other rival teachings, Confucian historians denigrated Shihuangdi as the arch villain of Chinese history. Legalism acquired a bad name, associated with unbridled power without any regard for moral constraints. As a result, traditional interpretations of Qin Shihuangdi almost always portrayed the First Emperor as a brutal dictator. Ideological antipathy toward the Legalist State of Qin was established early in the Confucian tradition, prior to its victory and formation of the first empire in 220 BCE. As early as 266 BCE, the Confucian philosopher Xunzi warned against it, and later Confucian historians universally denounced Shihuangdi. Their enmity was enlivened by the excesses of Shihuangdi's policies—he allegedly burned Confucian texts and buried Confucian scholars alive.

In the modern period, as the validity of Confucianism was called into question, different historical assessments of the first emperor began to emerge. Propelled by China's weakness in the latter half of the nineteenth and early twentieth century, Confucian tradition began to be regarded as a handicap to progress toward modernization. China's weakness in the face of foreign encroachments also caused some to look upon Shihuangdi with admiration. When foreign nations intruded upon Chinese territory, Kuomintang historians emphasized the role Shihuangdi played in repelling northern invaders, the construction of the Great Wall, calling him "one of the great heroes of Chinese history," and comparing him with the Kuomintang leader, Chiang Kai-shek.[8] Chiang mounted a Northern Expedition in the late 1920s, which led to the formation of a new nationalist government in Nanjing. Interpreters compared these initiatives to the unification brought about by Qin Shihuangdi.[9]

With the Communist victory in 1949 came a new assessment, one that initially refuted the Kuomintang historians. Following a Marxist critique, Shihuangdi's unification and standardization were interpreted in terms of ameliorating ruling- and merchant-class interests, not the nation or people. The fall of the Qin dynasty was seen favorably as the victory of the people through class struggle, as peasant rebellions in revolt against Shihuangdi's oppressive policies. Their victory, however, did not lead to a victory for Communism, as the peasant classes were deemed to remain complicit with the oppressive forces of landlords. In spite of this, many of Mao's own ruthless policies against so-called class enemies and counter-revolutionaries, including the disbanding of families (the mainstay of the Confucian social fabric), his attacks on intellectuals, and so on, invited comparison. A new wave of interpretation praising Shihuangdi as Mao's predecessor emerged in the 1970s.[10] In this new assessment, Qin Shihuangdi was praised for his ability to unify China against the forces of division and for his ruthless treatment of counter-revolutionaries. He was criticized, amazingly, for not being thorough enough and for allowing the forces of the old feudal order to continue after his death. This assessment paralleled Mao's own ruthless and thorough condemnation of class enemies during the Cultural Revolution. Mao, himself, weighed in on Qin Shihuangdi, in a classic display of oppressive zeal. "He buried 460 scholars alive; we have buried forty-six thousand scholars alive . . . You [intellectuals] revile us for being Qin Shi Huangs. You are wrong. We have surpassed Qin Shi Huang a hundredfold. When you berate us for imitating his despotism, we are happy to agree! Your mistake was that you did not say so enough."[11] Freed of any possible moral constraints that a Confucian tradition might impose, Mao was able to freely express his Legalist spirit, even if couched in the ideology of Marxism-Leninism. In 1973–74, the fervor for Legalist thought reached a crescendo in the Examining Legalist Theories and Censuring Confucianism movement, which has been described as an "exemplary incident of the pathological development of the Sinification of Marxism."[12] As in the case of Qin Shihuangdi, however, the excesses of Mao's brutal and repressive campaign proved too much to bear. With Mao's death in 1976, the Cultural Revolution came to an abrupt halt. The trial that followed of the Gang of Four, led by Mao's wife Jiang Qing, proved the final death knell of the Maoist movement.

Following a brief interim, the moderate faction of the CCP led by Deng Xiaoping seized control (for a discussion, see chapter 1). Deng initiated his policies of "opening up," implementing the so-called four modernizations (economy, agriculture, scientific and technological development, and national defense) and advancing an ambitious plan of opening and liberalizing the economy. In terms of the "dynastic cycle," Deng represents a move away from the ruthless autocratic ruler, toward an administrative style that emphasized bureaucratic centralism. The repressive actions sanctioned by Deng against the Tiananmen protestors in 1989, however, reveal the extent to which authoritarian measures remained possible in the exercise of CCP power and control. Mao's famous dictate, "power comes from the barrel of a gun,"[13] continued to represent the Party's response when facing opposition. Nonetheless, the era of economic progressivism initiated by Deng continued to hold sway in China, as Jiang Zemin and Hu Jintao followed Deng Xiaoping's pragmatic policies. Term limits were established, as were a new technocratic style of governance and a less centralized political structure (as introduced in the previous chapter). Outsiders contented themselves in the belief that China was easing toward a liberal democratic model.

With the assumption of power by Xi Jinping, China has entered its most recent iteration of CCP rule. As China moves further and further away from the war footing of its foundation, does the "dynastic cycle" and "bureaucratic cycle" of history foretell a move toward a more assured regime, content to rule through the arts of peace and cultural refinement (Confucianism), to forsake the brutality of oppression, the art of rule by force (Legalism)?

The Legalism of Xi Jinping

Xi Jinping's 2014 address to the Fifth Congress of the International Confucian Association in the Great Hall of the People gave great hope to Confucians within China and around the world that a new era was dawning, in which Confucius and the Confucian tradition would begin to reassume its historical role as a fixture, perhaps even a centerpiece of modern Chinese culture, reversing century-long initiatives to unseat and vilify it as the reason for China's decline. Many now see it as China's gift to the world and are diligently strategizing on ways to turn this aspiration into reality. To accomplish this, the reformulation efforts of New Confucians, as described in chapter 1, must first take hold in China itself.

Isn't Xi Jinping's announcement of the compatibility between CCP and Confucian values enough to substantiate the claim for a new era of Confucian ascendance? Perhaps, but an article by Sam Crane in the *Los Angeles Review of Books*, "Why Xi Jinping's China is Legalist, Not Confucian," explains succinctly why Xi Jinping's evocation of Confucianism should not be taken at face value.

Crane begins with a reference to Jiang Shigong, a law professor at Peking University, and one who believes that with Xi Jinping, China has entered an era of a new Confucian-Marxist leadership. He cites a recent article by Jiang—an explication of Xi's speech at the Nineteenth Party Congress in October 2017—where Jiang underplays Xi's Leninism with references to a variety of classical Chinese philosophical concepts, including "the unity of heaven and man"; "Learning of the Heart/Mind"; and "when the Way prevails, the world is shared by all," and so on. Typical of the new wave of Confucians, Jiang fails to see the assertion of Legalist principles hidden in Xi's proposals: "Jiang largely ignores the Legalist tradition of Chinese thought, which arguably has much greater relevance to the current emphasis on Party building and political centralization in the People's Republic of China. To paraphrase an old Maoist slogan,

Jiang is waving the Confucian flag to defeat the Confucian flag. In so doing, he is creating ideological space for an unspoken Legalist assertion of autocratic power."[14]

Crane goes on to assert that "the crux of that power is Xi Jinping himself, as supreme leader of a highly centralized, strictly disciplined, bureaucratic Party apparatus." Jiang argues that Xi's authority goes beyond Weberian categories of legal-rational and traditional authority to be a kind of "charismatic power," where Xi is the center of China both administratively and spiritually, "at the helm of a monocratic power structure that will carry out his interpretation of law and policy." This, in effect, makes Xi akin to a Chinese emperor in the Confucian tradition, whereby the position of ruler is not limited to political authority but assumes the role of spiritual leader as well, enacting a harmony between the three realms—heaven, earth, and human—the traditional role ascribed to a Chinese ruler (as *wang* 王) in Confucian terms. As Crane points out, it is the threat of disorder and collapse that weighs most heavily on the minds of Jiang Shigong and Xi Jinping, and it is this threat that is used as the rationale to justify harsh autocratic rule. Confucianism is not the buttress they lean on but rather Legalist theoreticians and administrators of the Warring States period who based their oppressive policies on the threat of disorder and chaos: "[L]ike Emperor Wu of the Han Dynasty, [Xi] reaches for Confucianism to serve as a pleasant façade to cover the unkinder reality of Legalist authoritarianism, advocating for 'integration of the rule of law and the rule of virtue.'"[15]

> Yet eager New Confucians, hopeful for a conversion of state ideology away from Marxism-Leninism, must take note of the clear limit Jiang sets against the "Confucianization of the Party," describing it as "the dregs of feudal restorationist thought." Jiang is not a Confucian. Xi Jinping is not a Confucian. They are, at base, Marxist-Leninists, working hard to strengthen a highly centralized authoritarian state under the leadership of an unassailable single leader. In that project they are enacting, in a modern context, not Confucianism nor any other humane Chinese philosophy, but the Legalist vision of Shang Yang and Han Feizi.[16]

The only thing I would add is to emphasize Crane's assessment of the implicit role Legalism has played throughout the Chinese tradition.

Humane government in China was always delivered in the shadow of absolute power. The ability of an emperor to express kindness and magnanimity was a function of the authority he assumed. This authority was buttressed by a Legalist foundation, even when unacknowledged, as it often was.

Han Feizi, quoted in the previous paragraph, was a prominent Legalist thinker whose ideas exerted extensive, if often unattributed, influence over China's Confucian tradition. Though not a Confucian himself, Han Feizi is tied to a Confucian pedigree through his teacher, Xunzi, the rival of Mencius discussed previously. Han Feizi built upon Xunzi's contention that humans are evil by nature and their propensity toward evil needs to be corrected. Whereas Xunzi invoked a regimen of ritual to train the evil nature toward goodness, Han Feizi called upon a strong state under absolutist rule to force people to refrain from evil—goodness considered an unattainable aim. His thinking provided a theoretical underpinning for a militaristic regime with heightened sensitivity to public security. Needless to say, individuals were only deemed worthy as they complied to state mandates, enforced through a strict code of rewards and punishments. Han Feizi's ideas were initially actualized by Qin Shihuangdi, the founder of the ruthless and short-lived Qin dynasty, revived by the Mao regime and today's Xi Jinping rule. The book of Han Feizi's writings written under the name of its author, was one of Chairman Mao's favorites and is repeatedly quoted by Xi Jinping.[17]

Xi himself, for his part, has taken a leading role in centralizing power in his own name and that of the Party. Although China imposed a two-term limit on its presidents in the 1990s, Xi recently had the limits removed through constitutional changes at the annual meeting of parliament, the National People's Congress, where all but five of the 2,969 delegates approved. This frees him to extend his tenure past the two-term limit, due to expire in 2023. To consolidate Xi's regime, the Congress enshrined "Xi Jinping Thought on Socialism with Chinese Characteristics for a New Era" in the constitution as its core principle. What the Xi administration envisages is a centralization of power whereby the government, military, and industry are orchestrated from the center to the periphery through strong and disciplined party leadership. The forms of this centralization, as outlined in a paper by Kazuko Kojima, include: (1) creation of a strong leader; (2) control of ideology and speech (including potential actors promoting Western values); (3) tightening of party discipline and organization through anticorruption campaigns, supervision, and inspection; (4) total control over everything by the Party; and (5) information control and the introduction of a credit rating system. Under point (5) for example, Article 9 of Internet Thread Comments Service Management Regulation (enacted in October 2017) requires providers to create a credit record that ranks users based on the content of their posts, to blacklist users who have posted content in violation of regulations, and to take disciplinary action, including account suspension. Similarly, the Cyberspace Information Office at the central and provincial levels is required to not only provide a credit record and a blacklist management system but also to make regular credit evaluations of providers. Other credit score systems have been introduced for industry governance.[18] Additional measures have been introduced to curb perceived excesses in other arenas, and there is widespread surveillance over the media and academia, not to mention religious organizations and minority groups.

Chapter Three

The Daoist Cycle of Life and the Way of Returning to the Fundamental

Millenarian Prophecy and the Environmental Movement in Contemporary China

Three Ways of Thought in Ancient China: How Did Confucianism, Legalism, and Daoism Influence Political Rule?

The patterns of rule in ancient China were informed by many traditions, the so-called Hundred Schools of Thought of the Spring and Autumn and Warring States periods (sixth century BC–221 BCE). Of the nascent schools of thought emerging during this time, three achieved long-lasting success: Confucianism, Legalism, and Daoism. Together, they form the triad of "three ways of thought in ancient China."[1] In outline form, we can see the contributions of each tradition.

For Confucianism, the pillar of rule lies in the *Junzi*, the moral exemplar, usually translated as the "Cultured Person," or "Superior Person," though these translations are inadequate to convey the commanding stature that the *Junzi* occupies. Through diligent effort, study, and training, the goal of becoming *Junzi* was an attainable one, exhibited in command over Confucian moral virtues: righteousness, reciprocity, loyalty, filial piety, and so on. Ultimately, the *Junzi* exhibited two leading qualities, *ren* (goodness, benevolence, or humaneness) and *li* (ritual propriety). The *Junzi* steeped in *ren* exhibited an internal attitude of altruism, directed at the betterment of oneself through the betterment of others. As a result, *ren* is regarded as the essence of humaneness, or what it means to be human, achieved through human interaction and shared experience. Human relations are at the core of *ren*, particularly family relationships that form the basis for human love and interactions, the source of the human self. *Li* originally indicated the actions associated with religious sacrifice but became a concept associated with a variety of meanings: ceremony, ritual, decorum, rules of propriety, good form, good custom, etc. According to commentators on the Confucian *Analects* like Herbert Fingarette, the association of *li* with its original meaning of religious sacrifice was retained, imbuing all human activity with an aura of sanctity.[2] Fingarette saw in this ability to transform secular encounters into sacred acts the leitmotif of Confucianism and its unique contribution to human culture. In conjunction with *li* there is the Confucian virtue of *yi*, often translated as righteousness, which is the ability to determine which action is correct. *Ren* is the inward expression of human virtue and the attitude to treat others in due course. *Li* is the outward expression or application of human virtue in action. The anticipated outcome of the program of virtue and virtuous conduct that Confucians encourage is an emergence of a sage: the paradigmatic Confucian ruler—a kind of enlightened philosopher-king who will realize the ideal Confucian society of peace, prosperity, and harmony. Confucians believe that such an ideal society once existed and seek its return through emulation of the sage kings of antiquity, the great heroes who initiated the principles of Chinese civilization on a Confucian model.

Legalism, as we saw in the previous chapter, advocated rule by an absolute monarch, not a sage. It put no trust in morality or human virtue. In contrast to the Confucian presupposition in innate human goodness, or at least that humans were reformable and could be made good, Legalists determined that human goodness could not be relied on. Human nature is innately avaricious and left to their own devices, humans breed competition and chaos. The only way to curb their greedy appetites was through laws and punishments. The threat of force and violence was necessary to ensure compliance with a strict regimen of rules and regulations. A strong state security apparatus watched over the populace to make sure rules and regulations were followed. A ruler with absolute authority presided over state and society, administering laws and punishments. A strong military supported by the ruler sought to enhance the state's wealth and prestige internationally through policies aimed at territorial expansion. The Legalists also parted ways with Confucians in their regard for the past. Legalists were pragmatists, not idealists. They did not believe in either rule by virtue or the hallowed principles of antiquity. Even if such a golden age existed in remote antiquity, they reasoned that the ways of the past have no relevance for the present. Times had changed; what worked in the past was no longer viable for current circumstances. New times demanded new methods. The tradition had no hold over them. While Legalism fell out of official favor with the ruthless policies of the Qin, its realpolitik approach to governing and its assumption of absolute power in an autocratic ruler continued to inform the policies of nominally Confucian regimes, as discussed in the last chapter, whereby Confucianism served "as a pleasant façade to cover the unkinder reality of Legalist authoritarianism."

The third way of thinking emanating from the Hundred Schools of Thought period of ancient China is Daoism, which is the focus of the current chapter. To understand the Daoist impact in China, I have chosen, in the first place, to situate it in the context of the "three ways of thought" to clarify its appeal. Its contemporary proponents fall within the shadow of this formative context, and the alternative vision they hold for China resonates with their Daoist forebears who looked to a different model for human civilization. Like the Confucians, Daoists also believed in a sage figure, but what a different model it was! The Daoist sage is an instinctive creature that is an embodiment of naturalness. This naturalness is not exhibited in the orchestrated human conduct of *li*, but in the processes of *yin* and *yang*, and the unimpeded operation of the "Way" (*dao*). Human society is not the natural manifestation of the *dao*, as Confucians pretend but an artificial creation that is but one option among many and, according to Daoists, a poor and unnatural approximation. A famous passage from the early Daoist text, the *Daode jing* (The Classic on the Way and its Virtue), articulates the way in which Daoists cast the emergence of Confucian teaching as a sign of the decline of civilization, not its affirmation. The Daoists assumed an ideal society in which the implicit, natural harmony of the *dao* prevailed. When this pristine state was lost, virtue (*de*) arose; when virtue was lost, humaneness (*ren*) arose; when humaneness was lost, righteousness (*yi*) arose; when righteousness was lost, ritual propriety (*li*) arose, ritual propriety being but a superficial expression of loyalty and faithfulness.[3] In one brief passage, the *Daode jing* castigated the whole program of Confucian virtue, reducing it to a shallow and perverted imitation of the true *dao*. With the Legalists, Daoists held no hope for human virtue, which they regarded as a Confucian fantasy. Another passage from the *Daode jing* stipulates, "Heaven and earth are not *ren* (humane): they treat the things of the world as straw dogs. The sage is not *ren*; he treats the world as straw dogs."[4] Straw dogs are ceremonial objects in ancient China, cast away once they have served their purpose. The *dao* operates in a similarly impartial manner; virtuous human conduct has no influence over the *dao*, one way or the other. How, then, should the sage act? What is it that he should do? In concert with heaven and earth, the sage rejects the hypothetical moral injunctions of the human realm and embodies the tangible virtue of spontaneity, or *wuwei*. Literally "non-action," *wuwei* does not actually call for "doing nothing," but for acting in perfect accordance with the forces of *yin* and *yang*. As opposed to the artifice created in accordance with deliberate human intentionality, *wuwei* represents a kind of "actionless action" that evinces an effortless and unselfconscious instinctuality. The ideal society in Daoism is sought through this primitive naturalism, where one anticipates the forces of *yin* and *yang* to be in rhythm with natural cycles, to be free of both inhibitions and hindrances, to display spontaneous freedom.

The *Dao* of the *Daode jing*: "Classic of the Way and Its Virtue/Power"

The concept *dao*, or Way, is not exclusive to Daoism but used in all traditions when referring to their teachings. In Daoism, however, *dao* takes on a central role that underscores its importance, and the way it is developed and articulated in the *Daode jing* speaks to its contemporary importance for China's incipient environmental movement.

The opening chapter of the *Daode jing* begins: "The *dao* that can be *dao'd* is not the eternal *Dao*. The name that can be named is not the eternal Name. As nameless, it is the origin of Heaven and Earth. As named, it is the mother of all things."[5] I have left the use of *dao* as a verb in the opening line untranslated. This "*dao'd*" is often rendered as "named," "spoken of," or "put into words," "understood," or "conceptualized." In short, it represents not the ultimate, cosmic *Dao*, but an application in time and space: a contextualized implementation. The same interpretation is applied to language. Whenever anything is "named" or "defined," it has left its cosmic, universal dimension, through its association with a concrete reality manifested in a particular form.

The "eternal *Dao*" and "eternal Name" cannot be described in words or designated by names. The *Dao/dao* is thus referred to in two aspects: "as nameless, it is the origin of Heaven and Earth; as named, it is the mother of all things." This *Dao/dao* distinction (made possible in English through capitalization) speaks to the nature of *Dao* in both its uncreated and created aspects. The opening chapter of the *Daode jing* also speaks to how passion and intentionality condition our understanding of *Dao/dao*. Free of desire, one observes the subtle *Dao*, the unseen, invisible principle that animates all existence. With desire, one observes the manifest *dao*, the appearances of *Dao* achieving realized form. "Both of these," the *Daode jing* goes on to assert, "derive from the same source; they have different names but the same designation." Even though we posit the *Dao/dao* distinction, this is an artificial imposition; the two represent a continuum, aspects of a single pattern. This is the "mystery of mysteries; the gate of all wonders."

Chapter 42 of the *Daode jing* provides further insight into the workings of the *Dao*, how *Dao* is actualized as *dao*, and how understanding and anticipating the workings of the *Dao* becomes possible. The chapter opens: "*Dao* gives birth to one; one gives birth to two; two gives birth to three; three gives birth to the myriad things." The "one" that cosmic, universal *Dao* gives birth to is primal *Qi*, the intrinsic, elemental force behind creation. It represents the gateway between the subtle, unseen realm of *Dao*, and the manifest reality of the time/space realm that we inhabit. The "two" that primal *qi* gives birth to are the elemental forces of *yin* and *yang*. The forces of *yin* and *yang* are variously understood as competing but complementary agents—dark and light, subtle and manifest, female and male, earth and heaven, and so on—that together produce the continuum between their two orbits. The "three" that gives birth to the myriad things are the two elemental forces of *yin* and *yang* coupled with what we may refer to as "applied *qi*" as distinct from primal *Qi* (again invoking English capitalization), created energy in contrast to its primal, essential form. This applied *qi* provides the impetus for *yin* and *yang* to commune with each other harmoniously, without conflict. Through this union, the myriad things are created; the world as it appears to us comes into being.[6] This sentiment is expressed in the concluding lines of the chapter: "The things of the world bear *yin* on their backs and embrace the *yang*. They exhaust their *qi* in harmony."

To anticipate the *Dao*, to be in harmonious step with it, one strives to understand its workings. Chapter 40 advises: "Reversal is the motion of the Dao. Weakness is the method of the Dao." To understand how

Dao works, one moves backward not forward, regressing rather than progressing. One unravels the mysterious processes through which eternal *Dao* (as the source of all things) becomes the myriad things (*dao* as manifested objects). Key to this process is the concept of *de*, which in the Confucian tradition refers to human moral virtue. Against ethical injunctions, the *de* in Daoism denotes the power of individuation, how *yin* and *yang* act in concert with *qi* to form the array of unique, created things that make up our world. *De* in Daoism is free of the moral judgment or righteousness (*yi*) required in Confucianism to enact the harmony of human society. To the contrary, in Daoism such an insertion of the human will is deemed as an artificial intrusion, an obstruction to the natural tendency of the *Dao*. Through *de* (as the power of individuation), the *Dao* produces an array of complements: being and nonbeing, difficult and easy, long and short, high and low, note and noise, before and after, etc.[7] Human involvement requires no more than to acknowledge and accept the relativity implicit in this array. Each opposite is but an indication of the continuum that the *Dao* fosters. Attempts to insert human judgment onto this continuum are a sham: "All in the world deem the beautiful to be beautiful; it is ugly. All deem the good to be good; it is bad."[8] Beauty and good are nothing more than a human construct—there is no absolute distinction to be made. Aesthetic and moral presumptions upon which cultures are founded are no more than human inventions. "Therefore," the *Daode jing* concludes, "the sage dwells in the midst of non-action (*wuwei*) and practices the wordless teaching."[9] Without acting or speaking, the sage causes no interference to the natural flow of the *Dao*. Or, by implication, when a situation calls on the sage to act or speak, he does so in a manner that anticipates and tallies with the spontaneous rhythm of existence the *Dao* has generated.

The cycle of existence that the *Dao* imposes serves as a natural law governing all created things. Once the duration of a thing's existence has run its course, it cycles back, or "returns" to a state of nonexistence, the realm of the Eternal *Dao* from whence the process repeats itself. In diagram form, the process may be depicted in figure 3.1.

One thing that has always struck me about this model of the workings of the *Dao* is the way it mimics the process of nature. In spring, shoots of plants miraculously emerge from the earth, produced from an unseen realm out of an apparent state of nonexistence. As chapter 40 further specifies: "The things of the world are born from being, and being is born of nothing." In summer, vegetation flourishes to produce

The Daoist Cycle of Life | 65

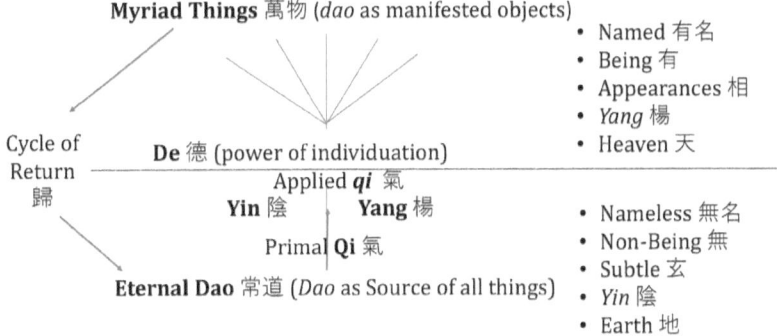

Figure 3.1. Diagram of the working of the Dao. Author provided.

an abundant array of flora. In fall, the verdant abundance of summer decays. By winter, it has died and returned to the earth from whence it rose. This agricultural model is apropos to a society like ancient and traditional China, where the cycle of the seasons dominated the rhythms of village life.

Ultimately, *Dao* is indefinable and only apprehended through its traces, its infinitely multiple aspects and appearances. *Dao* as a principle is at once transcendent and immanent: unnamable and ineffable, yet present in all things. *Dao* as "Way" is the principle underlying the change and transformation of all beings, the spontaneous process regulating the natural cycle of the universe. The world as it appears to us finds its unity through this process. The generative power of the *Dao*, *de*, is a creative power that is feminine. "One who knows the male but preserves the female becomes a ravine to the world. Such a one never swerves from constant individuating power (*de*) and returns again to be a newborn baby. . . . returns again to be an uncarved block."[10] To return to the generative force of nature is to embody the life-giving force of pure potentiality—the moment when all is possible before the creative process determines the course that individuated things will take. This is the magic moment, the fulcrum upon which creativity rests. To embody it, the sage rests in a constant state of *wuwei*. In the *Daode jing*, a series of metaphors are enlisted to point to the ineffability of *Dao*: the empty abyss as the inexhaustible ancestor of the world of things,[11] water that benefits all things and does not contend with them,[12] the nothingness at the center of spokes of a wheel, and individual vessels shaped from an amorphous clump of clay.[13] These metaphors indicate traces of *Dao*, indications of how *Dao* operates in the world we live in.

Throughout Chinese history, the philosophy of Daoism I have described has had relatively little impact on the execution of power in government. At times, the emperor is encouraged to imitate the manner of *wuwei* and allow his ministerial agents to exercise control over the actual levers of power while sitting aloof as the still center that animates the activity around him. In contemporary China, there is little talk of Daoist philosophy as a positive political force. Daoist religion is held in suspicion as supporting resentment and antigovernment sentiments. I discuss Religious Daoism and its potential impact separately, later in this chapter. The Daoism of the *Daode jing* has not been forgotten in China, however, and is beginning to enjoy a revival through an incipient environmental movement, one that sees in Daoism the seeds of China's environmental renaissance.

The Way of Returning to the Fundamental: The "Green Dao" in Contemporary China

Of China's traditions, Daoism has had the most difficulty adapting to modern circumstances. Long associated with individual (even libertarian) freedom, Daoism inspires spontaneous expression that appeals to artists but draws the ire of autocrats and bureaucrats who are not inclined to tolerate its unrestricted vitality. Moralists, too, are unimpressed with Daoism's disregard for ethical standards and conventional norms. Even more damning is the historical association between institutional Daoism and antigovernment resistance, especially at the local level. This aspect of Daoism is considered in more detail later in this chapter. In spite of the obstacles that prevent Daoism from finding relevance in contemporary China, it has found a place among Chinese environmentalists for its call to respect and acknowledge the cycles of nature and the ecological disasters accompanying China's rapid industrialization.

According to a recent report, humanity has wiped out 60 percent of animal populations since 1970, leading the world's foremost experts to warn that the annihilation of wildlife is now an emergency that threatens civilization.[14] As has been well documented, China is among the world's leading polluters,[15] highlighting a plethora of environmental issues that have emerged as China modernizes. These issues have had a serious deteriorating effect on the nation's biophysical environment and human health. Rapid large-scale industrialization and lax environmental oversight combine to foster mounting ecological problems. The associated health problems are negatively affecting the Chinese populace and contributing significantly to the build-up of greenhouse gases that contribute to climate change. Yet, the situation is not all bleak, and I, for one, believe that these are issues China is currently confronting.

The Center for American Progress, a liberal public policy and advocacy organization based in Washington, DC, described China's environmental policy in 2012 as similar to that of the United States before 1970. In both cases, the central government mandates fairly strict regulations, but actual monitoring and enforcement are largely undertaken by local governments that are more interested in fostering economic growth than environmental regulation. In addition, because of restrictive activities by China's government, the environmental work of nongovernmental forces, such as lawyers, journalists, and nongovernmental organizations, is seriously handicapped.[16] Against this laxity of enforcement, however, has emerged some significant pushback from the Chinese citizenry. Complaints to environmental authorities have shown signs of significant increase, and the director of the Institute of Public and Environmental Affairs, Ma Jun, reported in 2007 an increase of 29 percent in the number of mass protests caused by environmental issues, every year since 2002.[17] The Chinese government has understandably taken notice and has become increasingly concerned about issues relating to the environment and fostering ecologically sensitive economic growth. Premier Wen Jiabao, in a 2007 address, repeatedly referenced the "environment," "pollution," and "environmental protection," calling for stricter environmental regulations. While the results were mixed and some environmental targets were subsequently missed, this represented a turning point in the Chinese government's attitude toward enforcing environmental policies. Even so, China has had difficulty executing a policy that manages the advantages of economic growth against negative environmental impacts. Polluting industries continued to receive incentives, while the forces of corruption hindered effective enforcement, as local authorities ignored orders from the central government. In 2014 China amended its protection laws for the first time since 1989 to help fight pollution and reverse environmental damage in the country.[18]

As mentioned in chapter 1, official CCP policy currently aims at China becoming an "ecological civilization" (*shengtai wenming*). This eco-civilizational agenda is now a driving force in many areas of the People's Republic of China (PRC) environmental and renewable energy policies that are being implemented and funded. As R. James Ferguson has recently noted, the PRC government recognizes the cost of environmental degradation of recent years in response to rising energy needs and societal expectations unleased through the promises of the "Chinese Dream." It has linked large segments of economic, energy, developmental, and social and foreign-relations policy under the integrated rubric of a "harmonious society" and "harmonious world" doctrine. This approach was explicitly endorsed under Xi Jinping in 2013–2018, and the construction of an ecological civilization was given the status of a national development strategy, included in the Thirteenth Five-Year Plan for 2016–2020. Behind the debate stands the long-term engagement of Chinese civilization with its environmental and productive base. Early Chinese dynasties were renowned as pioneers in irrigation and agricultural expansion and developed philosophies directly supportive of agriculture as the "root" on which the other branches of society and the state were established. But as Ferguson notes, the difficulty of maintaining a large peasant (farming) population on the land without excessive human and environmental exploitation became a major dilemma for all imperial dynasties. This tension today finds expression in the challenge of providing food security and rural livelihoods during periods of intensified industrialization and urbanization, with large segments of the population leaving agriculture for employment opportunities in urban industries. This will continue to be one of the major challenges for a truly ecological civilization in the twenty-first century, in China as elsewhere.[19]

The back-and-forth nature of environmental reform in China may not be unusual. The rising wealth and economic expectations of China's populace is difficult to manage, and inhibitors to continued growth are bound to be met with protest in some quarters. On the other hand, environmental devastation in China is real, as are the debilitating effects it has on the health of Chinese people. Amid calls for a "Green G.D.P.,"[20] an index of economic growth with the environmental consequences of that growth factored in, one also witnesses a rise of

"Green Dao" environmental movements in contemporary China that invoke hallowed and ancient Daoist teachings in an attempt to reverse the tide of environmental devastation.

Indicative of the trend in contemporary Daoism to associate the *Dao* with environmental activism is the movement on Mao-shan, or Mount Mao. A recent report by Javier C. Hernández, "Mao Mountain Journal," documented this movement, spearheaded by Abbot Wang of Chongxi Wanshou (Sublime joy of everlasting life) Temple on Mount Mao (also known as Mount Difei).[21] Abbot Yang has grown frustrated by China's indifference to a crippling pollution crisis that has devastated the land and marred the sky. In reaction, Wang erected a $17.7 million eco-friendly temple, opened in August 2016, and cites teachings inspired by the ancient texts of Daoism to call for a change in course for China. "China doesn't lack money," Wang declares, "it lacks a reverence for the environment," adding that Chinese morals are in decline, and traditional beliefs have been lost. Wang calls for a return to China's roots as an ecological civilization. The processes of the *Dao* espoused in the *Daode jing* are the roots to which Wang and similarly inspired environmental activists demand a return. Wang's aspirations are in line with President Xi, who has championed the return of Chinese traditions to help foster the Chinese dream, which invokes a return to China's roots as an ecological civilization—a vision Xi has reportedly described as having "clear waters and green mountains" across the land.

The Chongxi Wanshou Temple on Mount Mao comprises twenty acres, including an organic vegetable garden and a giant statue of Laozi, the founder of Daoism and alleged author of the *Daode jing* (see figure 3.2 on next page), who is worshiped as a "green god." The mountain's spiritual leaders seek to define a distinctly Chinese type of environmentalism, one that emphasizes harmony with nature instead of Western notions of "saving the earth," and Daoist officials have also spoken up at national leadership meetings in recent years, calling on the government to take more action to prevent environmental catastrophes.[22]

There is some irony in the development of the "Green Dao" movement. It is the product of increased wealth in China, which has provided resources for China's religious revival among a population eager for spiritual and religious sustenance among the excesses of material culture. This same return to religion fuels environmental awakening, especially in (but not limited to) Daoism, as people find alternate principles and meanings in their lives, divorced from material acquisition fueled

Figure 3.2. A monumental statue at Mt. Qingyuan of Lao-Tzu, the Chinese philosopher who lived c. 500 BCE and credited with founding Daoism (Taosim). Courtesy of Thanato via WikiCommons.

by uninhibited economic growth. In the wake of China's attempted "greening," religious followers are initiating organizations to serve as watchdogs against polluters and using their faith to protest plans to build factories and power plants near their homes.[23]

While the Daoist environmental movement seems small, it harbors unforeseeable potential. Revolutionary protest movements in China have regularly erupted from such humble beginnings.

The "Other Side" of the Dao: Religious Daoism as Revolutionary Force

In practice, Daoism developed an institutional religious framework related to but quite different than its ancient textual tradition. In Chinese, this Daoism is known as Dao-jia, the "Family of the Dao," in contrast to the textual tradition or Dao-jiao, the "Teaching of the Dao." The textual tradition, based on Laozi's *Daode jing* and the *Zhuangzi*, became known in the West as "Philosophical Daoism," while the "Family of the Dao" was referred to as "Religious Daoism." Religious Daoism has hypothetical origins in Chinese shamanism, in the belief that gods, demons, ancestral spirits, etc., work for the good or ill of humans through the medium of its emissaries (i.e., shamans). In ancient China, it was known as the Huang-Lao Dao, "the Way of the Yellow Emperor and Laozi." It fell out of favor with the official establishment of Confucianism as the state ideology by Emperor Wu (r. 141–87 BCE) of the Han dynasty but became the basis for nonofficial liturgical organizations at local levels. As such, it served a vital role in the political dynamics of Chinese history as the basis for the classic split in authority (and sometimes conflict) between central administration (Confucian) and local organizations (Daoist). In its capacity for local representation, it became the vehicle for antigovernment resistance and protest. In extreme situations whereby government policies regarding taxation, conscription, corvée labor, etc., were deemed intolerable, local Daoist organizations formed a basis for messianic and millenarian movements. Typical of these were the so-called Taiping movements aimed at establishing a reign of Great Peace (*taiping*) that hypothetically existed before civilization and were destined to reappear on earth. These movements were inspired through revelations to millenarian leaders who frequently became commanders of armed insurrections that pressed for change, including the revolutionary overthrow of dynastic leaders. In this way, the Daoist religion was provided the pretext for dynastic overthrow, as suggested in the dynastic cycle in the previous chapter. In the absence of democratic processes, revolution is the mechanism for government change, and Daoist-based insurrections become the instrument of political transformation.

In the twentieth century, the CCP was the mechanism for a popular revolution that produced political change. Centered around a strong, charismatic leader in Mao Zedong, the Party embodied the aspirations of the masses and formed an organization capable of toppling the unpopular fledgling government of Republican China, led by Chiang Kai-shek. Embedded within Marxist ideology is a millenarian message of creating a classless, harmonious, and ethically just society: a utopian socialism. While the dream of a Daoist-based reign of "great peace" is at present but a distant prospect, without a mechanism for peaceful political transition, the prospect for revolutionary upheaval in China remains, as does a Daoist role for its inspiration. In short, the dynastic cycle is predicated on the inevitability of ultimately violent political change. The dynastic cycle is but a manifestation of the "workings of the *Dao*," which depicts the inevitable rise and fall of created things. Without heeding this underlying message of the *Dao* and calling for more peaceful and measured transformations, presumptions of political authority in contemporary China remain subject to a similar fate.

The prospects of popular protest have not diminished in contemporary China. The number of Daoist temples, like religious institutions more generally, has risen spectacularly in the tolerant and prosperous period following Deng Xiaoping's reforms. Regardless of inspiration, protest seems to have a healthy present and future. In the decades since the death of Mao Zedong, a wide variety of protests and dissident movements have arisen. While the most notable ones, like the Tibetan uprising in 1959, the Tiananmen Square protests in 1989, the demonstration by Falun Gong practitioners at Zhongnanhai in 1999, have captured international attention, these pale in number to the protests and demonstrations mounted by the Chinese citizenry over a wide range of issues, including corruption, forced evictions, unpaid wages, human rights abuses, environmental degradation, ethnic protests, petitioning for religious freedom and civil liberties, protests against one-party rule, as well as nationalist protests against foreign countries. These rose especially in the period of increased tolerance, basically the era initiated by Deng Xiaoping's rule in the 1980s through the advent of Xi Jinping's rule in 2012. According to reports, there were approximately 8,700 "mass group incidents" in 1993,[24] and these had risen tenfold to 87,000 in 2005.[25] In 2010, Chinese sociology professor Sun Liping estimated the number of incidents at 180,000.[26] In spite of this seemingly overwhelming number of protests, scholars caution that they do not yet pose an existential threat to Communist Party rule, as they lack "connective tissue" to develop into a massive systematic challenge.[27] The majority of protests and demonstrations in China are carried out at the regional level, aimed at local grievances, and do not seek systematic change.[28]

It is unclear at this juncture when and where the "connective tissue" calling for systematic change might come from. The Communist Party's hold on power seems secure, and Xi Jinping's recent repressive policies have further undermined and delegitimized any incipient forces of protest in China. The status quo is liable to remain strong as long as the economy keeps expanding, wealth continues to rise, and more and more people are raised out of poverty, not to mention the increasing power and prestige that China commands on the world stage. China's current territorial boundaries rival the Chinese empire at its most expansive period (although Taiwan remains a sticking point). The Belt and Road Initiative (considered in a later chapter) pushes the extent of China's international reach to its historical limit and beyond. This has resulted in great pride among the Chinese citizenry, who revel in their good fortune and China's prestige after the long "era of humiliation" suffered at the hands of international powers in the nineteenth and twentieth centuries. For the moment, the likelihood of a challenge to Communist Party authority is not strong, but economic cycles predict that China's current largesse, fueled by decades of double-digit growth, cannot last forever. When economic decline comes, as it inevitably will, forces may rise to challenge the Party's grip on power. In the interim, the Party remains vigilant. Like imperial regimes before it, the Party keeps a close watch on society for potential signs of unrest. Natural disasters, earthquakes, floods, and famines retain their potential for social disruption, not to mention any prospect for war, which could bring an era of chaos like those visited upon China in the past. China has had no battlefield experience since the Sino-Vietnamese War of 1979, which lasted a mere four weeks. While the victor in the conflict is disputed (in Vietnam, it is known as the "War against Chinese Expansionism"; In China, it is referred to as the "Defensive Counterattack against Vietnam"), most Western observers concluded that Vietnamese forces outperformed the People's Liberation Army (PLA) on the battlefield.[29] Regardless of tactical and operational limitations of the PLA, China did achieve its geopolitical and strategic goals in relation to Cambodia and limiting Vietnam's role in Southeast Asia, even when backed by the Soviets.

While China has striven to upgrade its military to a formidable force, performance in actual combat situations remains untested. What is certain is the vaguely conceived "will of the people" needed for a Chinese government's ability to rule. This is a principle first issued from the ancient Confucian writer, Mencius, second only to Confucius in the Confucian pantheon of sages. *"The people are to be valued most, the altars of the grain and the land [traditional symbols of the vitality of the state] next, the ruler least. Hence winning the favor of the common people* you become Emperor" (7B14, emphasis mine). Mencius famously argued that it is acceptable for the subjects to overthrow or even kill a ruler who ignores the people's needs and rules harshly. A ruler who does not rule justly is no longer a true ruler. While ideas of what constitutes just rule are no longer dominated by Confucian criteria, contemporary Chinese governments continue to be evaluated according to standards such as this.

As a one-party state that tolerates no political opposition, China and the CCP are subject to the historical dynamics associated with all authoritarian regimes. In terms of the Chinese Dynastic Cycle, the fate of such regimes can only be ultimately decided by revolution. Lacking a mechanism for the peaceful evolution of power, the fate of regimes is decided through bloodshed and chaos. Xi's attempt to impose Legalistic types of remedies to control society in the name of Party discipline and social cohesion is but a manifestation of the true nature of the regime, the success of which is a question that only the future can determine.

Chapter Four

The Return of the Nonnative
The Buddhist Revival in Contemporary China

The Clash between Confucian Morality and Buddhist Enlightenment

Among the most surprising developments of China's rise is the revival of Buddhism. Only the return of the native, Confucius, rivals the revival of Buddhism as the most astonishing development of the post-Mao era. The contemporary Buddhist revival in China is remarkable on two counts: (1) it is a religion, perhaps China's most deeply rooted; and (2) it has historically struggled to be included as a Chinese tradition, being relegated to foreign status based on its nonnative origins. Count (1) is remarkable given the CCP's Marxist orientations and its aims to extricate religion as a blight and to create a society free of the fanciful and false dreams that religion is based on. Count (2) is remarkable given that China's experience with Buddhism extends over two thousand years and that Buddhism has been an important contributor to Chinese culture and civilization as long as Christianity has in the West. Because of count (2), the CCP's assessment of Buddhism and its desire to eradicate it is not new but has a long history in the Chinese context.

At the end of the Tang dynasty (618–906), a period often referred to as a "golden age" when China was dominated by Buddhist thought and institutions, a strident Confucian voice emerged to challenge the Buddhist influence on society. Han Yu advocated a return to the "golden age" of antiquity and the principles of ancient Confucian Chinese civilization. He promoted a revival of "classical style" (*guwen*) writing, simple and direct, modeled on the prose works of antiquity, as best suited to communicate ancient values. And he attacked Buddhism as antithetical to native Chinese cultural values. His arguments were put forth in the essay "Memorial on the Bone of the Buddha," written to the emperor on the occasion of a great Buddhist celebration to commemorate the alleged relic of the Buddha paraded through the streets of the capital. In "Memorial," Han Yu alleged that the Buddha was "barbarian" and that before the arrival of his teachings in the golden age of the past, the empire was in a state of perfect equilibrium. As the worship of Buddhism increased, dynasties became more short-lived. The Tang dynasty's founding emperor had sought to eradicate Buddhism only to have his plan thwarted by pro-Buddhist advisors. According to Han Yu, it is a travesty, given the founder's intention, that the current emperor allows for a procession of the bone of the Buddha even into the precincts of the imperial palace to be worshiped. The example the emperor sets, contends Han Yu, confuses common people and encourages worship of the Buddha, resulting in numerous destructive, superstitious practices. Han Yu concludes that the emperor should under no circumstances allow the relic into the palace; it should be destroyed.

The Buddha was an inappropriate model for emulation, according to Han Yu, because he was born a barbarian (i.e., not a native Chinese) and knew nothing of Confucian virtues, such as loyalty and filial piety. While Han Yu's views were considered extreme in the Tang dynasty, they became more mainstream, if contested, in succeeding centuries. They eventually formed the orthodox position of the Confucian revival, Neo-Confucianism, especially the central tradition of Zhu Xi's School of Principle. Confucians had long contested the Buddhist presence in China, railing against the economic costs of supporting the Buddhist clergy who were deemed an "extra class" in addition to craftsmen, peasant farmers, the Confucian ruling elite, and the dreaded but tolerated merchants that comprised the ideal Confucian society. Supporting the Buddhists provided no tangible benefits to society, according to Confucians, but constituted an economic burden that strained limited resources. Also, as Buddhist monastic estates thrived, they became repositories of wealth, housing countless treasures, precious metals and gems, in addition to lands and business enterprises and the people who worked them.

Coupled with the economic impact that Buddhism had, Confucian-minded Chinese were upset over the social and moral violations that

Buddhist teaching invoked. The Buddhist clergy in China remained unmarried and as such were unable to fulfill the cardinal Confucian obligation of producing offspring, especially male offspring, who could perpetuate the family lineage, look after parents in old age, and offer sacrifices to them when deceased. The entire Confucian moral system was predicated on human relationships, and the decision to not contribute was seen as a violation of a social order inscribed by Heaven. The Buddhist quest for nirvana, enlightenment, or an afterlife of bliss, was viewed as a selfish, individualistic goal not in keeping with Confucian aspirations for a society that worked in harmony toward the good of the collective. One way of depicting the discrepancy between the aims of Buddhism and those of Confucianism is to review the two programs of development and the means of attaining the goals proposed by each: the Buddhist Noble Eightfold Path and the Confucian program of Great Learning.

The Buddhist Noble Eightfold Path is the fourth of the Four Noble Truths, the résumé of Buddhist teaching allegedly delivered by Śākyamuni in his sermons, dedicated to the path (using the Chinese word *dao*, or "Way") leading to the realization of the goal of nirvana.

Noble Eightfold Path: Three Components

Right Understanding Wisdom
Right Intention(*prajñā*)

Right Speech Moral Conduct
Right Action (*śila*)
Right Livelihood

Right Effort Mental Discipline
Right Mindfulness (*samādhi*)
Right Concentration

While the eightfold path is normally depicted as the eight spokes of the wheel that turns the dharma, or Buddhist teaching, these spokes are built on the base of a tripartite hub. The three components of this hub—wisdom, moral conduct, and mental discipline—form the themes that animate the Buddhist path and one's progress on it.

The Confucian program of development is summarized in an influential essay, "Great Learning," in the *Book of Rites*, one of the five classic texts of early Confucianism. With the advent of Neo-Confucianism in the Song dynasty (960–1278), the essay was singled out for inclusion in a new and more concise canon for Confucian learning and training, the "Four Books." As a result, the topic of "Great Learning" became prominent in the Confucian curriculum of study and practice, the aim of which was to become a *junzi*, or Confucian cultivated person, the exemplar of Confucian virtue and judgment.

Confucian Program of Development in the Great Learning

1. Investigate things
2. Extend knowledge
3. Make thoughts sincere
4. Rectify the mind
5. Develop the self
6. Manage the family
7. Govern the state
8. Have peace prevail throughout the land

The program of Great Learning entails, first, development involving investigating phenomena and developing knowledge, moral resolve and individual integrity (stages 1 through 5). Then, the individual integrity developed is applied to critical social engagements: managing the family (stage 6), governing the state (stage 7), and pacifying the empire (stage 8). On one level, the lofty aspirations of the Great Learning are aimed at an elite few who lead the empire and direct affairs of state. At a more general level, the implications of the Great Learning influence everyone in society who belongs to a family or clan unit.

While the early Buddhist development program had been altered somewhat by the time Buddhism reached China, it was still indicative of the broad aims that the tradition aspired to, at least in the eyes of its Confucian detractors. To them, the Buddhist plan, although encouraging the development of wisdom and insight, moral training, and mental discipline, was aimed at a self-centered fantasy, nirvana, that contributed nothing substantial to social well-being. On the contrary, it encouraged practitioners to forgo social responsibilities, to discard loyalty for altruism and filial piety for self-obsession.

The Buddhist Revival in Contemporary China

During the Mao period, religious expression was severely curtailed in China, culminating in the Cultural Revolution, where religion in China ceased to exist as a visible force. Christian churches, Muslim mosques, Daoist temples, and Buddhist monasteries were either destroyed or, more commonly, repurposed for "useful" functions. When I visited China in the 1980s, there were only meager signs of religious revival. In Hangzhou, where Chinese culture is practically synonymous with Chinese Buddhist culture, only the fabled Lingyin Monastery was functioning. Three affiliated monasteries, Upper, Middle, and Lower Tianzhu, each important in their own right, had been repurposed. One was being used as a factory, one was used as a residence for locals, and one was completely inaccessible. The one used as a residence bore the scars of the turmoil that the Cultural Revolution had wrought. Inside the main hall, the altar where the principal image for worship once stood was decimated. Smoke stains scarred the room. On one wall, a stenciled slogan of a saying from Chairman Mao was painted in bright red (see figure 4.1 on next page).

The slogan was repurposed by Red Guard bands from a speech delivered by Mao to the CCP's National Conference on Propaganda Work, March 12, 1957, to serve as a call for the destruction of institutions propagating the Four Olds—old customs, old culture, old habits, and old ideas—a campaign that began shortly after the launch of the Cultural Revolution in 1966. Buddhist and other religious institutions were prime targets for this destruction as purveyors of old customs, culture, habits, and ideas, especially to the extent that they were based on fallacies and superstitious practices. The goal of the campaign was extermination: to rid society of its religious and spiritual proclivities so that the new socialist dawn, guided by dialectical materialism, could emerge.

The Cultural Revolution was not the first time China had turned against Buddhism (and religion more generally, especially Daoism), in a quest to rid society of so-called fallacious ideas and superstitious practices. Criticism of Buddhism in China emerged soon after its introduction from India and Central Asia, and these critiques at times turned

80 | The Future of China's Past

Figure 4.1. "All erroneous ideas, all poisonous weeds, all ghosts and monsters, must be subjected to criticism; in no circumstance should they be allowed to spread unchecked." Photo by author, 1985.

into diatribes, not unlike the extremes witnessed during the Cultural Revolution. Chinese Buddhists' retelling of their history often note Four Great Persecutions:

1. Emperor Wu of Northern Wei (446)
2. Emperor Wu of Northern Zhou (574/7)
3. Emperor Wuzong of Tang (841–845)
4. Emperor Shizong of Later Zhou (955)

These persecutions were conducted for economic and socio-moral reasons mentioned previously. They typically involved the appropriation of monastic property and possessions, the closing of monasteries, and the forced return of clergy to lay life, positive social relations, and productive labor. A few officially designated monasteries were allowed to remain open in each circuit or province, staffed with a specific number of clergy (e.g., thirty or fifty). In this way, Buddhist prestige, social influence, and economic power, having risen to a point that threatened imperial governments, were reined in. The charge that Buddhism fostered fallacious ideas and superstitious practices served as a leading justification for suppression.

Aside from major persecutions, Buddhism existed in China within an uneasy context of court rivalries among proponents of the three major traditions (either devoted solely to one or in some kind of combination): Confucianism, Daoism, and Buddhism. This meant that imperial policy fluctuated according to the whims of those wielding power and the contentions of those who vied for it. As a result, policies toward Buddhism, pro, anti, or neutral, were in constant flux, always subject to change. This environment bred Buddhists who were vigilant and resilient, willing and able to capitalize on connections with literati supporters and foster undercurrents of popular support that existed in society.

Viewed from the perspective of the Four Great Persecutions, Buddhist resiliency exhibited itself in the revivals that followed in their wake.

Pattern of Buddhist Suppressions and Revivals in China

1. Emperor Wu of Northern Wei (446)

    → Emperor Wencheng restoration (454)

2. Emperor Wu of Northern Zhou (574/7)

    → Emperor Yang of Sui restoration (581–618)

3. Emperor Wuzong of Tang (841–845)

    → Emperor Xuanzong restoration (846)

4. Emperor Shizong of Later Zhou (955)

    → Early Song Emperors restoration (960–1022)

After each of the persecutions, a revival followed that attempted (and often succeeded) in returning Buddhism to its former glory. This pattern of suppression and revival represents the key dynamic of the Buddhist experience in China, vacillating between a thriving institution and the threat of extinction.

The success of Song dynasty administrative reforms toward Buddhism alleviated the need for any major persecution after the tenth century. Buddhism existed in the contentious climate described above, with policies vacillating between pro, anti, and neutral. The Confucian revival effectively "tamed" Buddhism, allowing it a marginal and supporting role but depriving it of any pretext for dominance. This does not mean that Buddhism was not subjected at times to massive destruction. The Taiping Rebellion and the warfare and chaos that prevailed at the end of the Qing dynasty in the nineteenth and early twentieth centuries reduced many Buddhist institutions to rubble. Whatever recovery was possible was interrupted by the Communist victory in 1949, and the extermination campaign referred to above with the excesses of the Great Proletarian Cultural Revolution (1966–1976). The Taiping campaign of destruction and the Cultural Revolution may be counted among the great Buddhist persecutions in Chinese history. The advent of moderate policies with Deng Xiaoping's ascension to party leader following the death of Mao included religious tolerance. The contemporary revival of Buddhism thus echoes the pattern of earlier suppression and revival dynamics.

Great Proletarian Cultural Revolution (1966–1976)

→ CCP tolerance toward Buddhism as a legitimate aspect of Chinese culture

Buddhism in China is currently in the throes of a great renaissance as it struggles to gain a footing in the new environment. Despite Xi Jinping's recent reluctance to embrace religion, Buddhism continues to enjoy government support, even with added restrictions. What are the parameters governing the current Buddhist revival? How is CCP tolerance manifest in the development of Buddhism and Buddhist institutions in post-Mao China?

A Tale of Two Stūpas:
The Parameters of Buddhist Revival in Contemporary China

The revival of Buddhism is so widespread that it is impossible to encapsulate it all. In the following, I discuss the revival with a focus on the region I am most familiar with, the greater Hangzhou region, including Ningbo and much of Zhejiang province. Hangzhou is a cultural center in China with a long and illustrious history. Hangzhou served as the imperial capital of China during the Southern Song dynasty (1127–1279) and has long been a focal point for the development of southern Chinese culture. Marco Polo, in his *Travels*, described it as the finest and most luxurious city in the world. Some verses from a poem by Ouyang Xiu, famous Neo-Confucian writer and administrator, describe an atmosphere likely applicable to the city.

Spring Day on West Lake

The lovely Spring breeze has come
Back to the Lake of the West
The Spring waters are so clear and
Green they might be freshly painted.
The clouds of perfume are sweeter
Than can be imagined. In the
Gentle East wind the petals
Fall like grains of rice.[1]

The region is one of the strongholds of Buddhism, both historically and at present. While Hangzhou remains the capital of Zhejiang Province, it has been overshadowed in the region by the development of Shanghai, now a mega-city that was initially established in the nineteenth century according to treaty terms in the aftermath of the Opium War. The Buddhist character of Hangzhou city and region is still intact, and Buddhist monuments and institutions, while significantly fewer in number than before, continue to dominate the cultural heritage.

Two monuments in the city of Hangzhou represent parameters to consider as dimensions of the contemporary Buddhist revival. The monuments are both funerary mounds—or stūpas (*ta* in Chinese). Buddhist stūpas originated in India as dome-shaped monuments used to commemorate the Buddha. Before its encounter with Indo-Greek culture (developed in the wake of Alexander the Great's conquest) in the Gandharan region of what is now northwestern Pakistan, Indian Buddhist culture did not worship likenesses of the Buddha in human form. The ancient Greeks, as we know, were quite comfortable carving human likenesses of their gods and as the Indo-Greek community converted to Buddhism, they continued their habit with depictions of the Buddha and

Buddhist deities. Cast in bronze and stone, many of these images have survived and are present in many art galleries and museums throughout the world. Prior to these developments in Gandhara, Indian Buddhist culture commemorated the Buddha by worshiping his relics (śarīra), stored in containers and buried beneath dome-shaped mounds. According to tradition, after the parinirvana (the final nirvana, or death) of the Buddha, his remains were cremated, and ashes were encased in urns and buried under eight mounds (divided among eight monarchs of the day).

After King Aśoka (304–232 BCE) united much of the Indian subcontinent and founded the Maurya dynasty, he converted to Buddhism and became dedicated to spreading its teachings throughout his land. As part of his efforts, tradition records that Aśoka gathered the remains of the Buddha dispersed in the urns buried under the eight mounds and instructed a Buddhist elder to miraculously cover the sun with his hand while the relics were instantaneously dispersed throughout the world in eighty-four thousand urns. This number is not arbitrary but was believed to represent the number of atoms comprising the human body. Through this act, Aśoka symbolically reconstituting the sacred body of the Buddha, resurrecting it throughout the world. The Buddha's remains transformed the substratum of the world into the sacred realm of the Buddha, a "living stūpa or "Buddha-land," demarcated literally as the body of the Buddha. One of Aśoka's stūpas, as luck would have it, is located in Ningbo, a short distance from Hangzhou. The sacred Buddha-relic allegedly housed at this location is the key attraction of a complex that bears Aśoka's name, Ayuwang (King Aśoka) monastery. It is one of the major Buddhist institutions in the region and figured prominently in the development of Buddhism (see figure 4.2).

During the tenth century, during the interregnum between the Tang and Song dynasties, a period known as the Five Dynasties and Ten Kingdoms, a local kingdom with its capital in Hangzhou (then known as Qiantang) became a prominent haven for Buddhist monks. The kingdom, known as Wuyue, developed the vibrant Buddhist culture that marks the region down to the present. The king who ruled Wuyue during its peak, King Qian Chu, like many devoted Buddhist rulers before him, strove to emulate the model of Aśoka by dispersing his own set of eighty-four thousand urns containing the Buddha's relics throughout his kingdom, thus marking it as a Buddha-land. By this time, the Buddha's remains comprised two types: corporeal or physical remains (rupa-kāya), and the sutras preached by the Buddha (dharma-kāya) were deemed as

Figure 4.2. King Aśoka Stūpa in Ningbo, China. Photo by author.

the essence of the Buddha himself. Among Qing Chu's miniature stūpas constructed to house Buddha's remains (see figure 4.3 on next page), were ones housed in a prominent pagoda overlooking West Lake, known as Leifeng (Thunder peak) Pagoda. It was constructed between 971 and 977 at the order of Qian Chu, to celebrate the birth of a son by one of his favorite concubines, named Huang Fei, and was originally known as Huangfei Pagoda. The pagoda was constructed with Buddhist sutras written on the foundation bricks, meant to protect the Buddhist relics buried under the structure from evil.

The pagoda became a household name in China thanks to the popular folk tale, "The Legend of the White Snake," a touching story

86 | The Future of China's Past

Figure 4.3. King Aśoka style stūpa unearthed from Leifeng Pagoda ruins. Photo by author.

about a girl who changed into a snake and her lover, a young man. As the pagoda deteriorated over time, people often took bricks from the pagoda in the belief that the abrasive powder of the bricks was a magic remedy that could cure all diseases and keep a fetus from aborting. People also stole the foundation bricks of the pagoda for other reasons. Many believed that the gold-colored bricks would bring them wealth. Also, owing to the legend of Madam White Snake, the pagoda was believed to have the power to repel snakes. In Hangzhou, where the silk industry has long flourished, many stole the foundation bricks in the belief that these would protect their silkworms from snakes. It was also ravaged by Japanese pirates during the Ming dynasty (1368–1644) when the region was unprotected. Finally, in August 1924, the pagoda collapsed. Lu Xun, the famous author and prominent figure in the New Culture movement who laid the foundations for modern Chinese literature, wrote an essay commenting on the collapse of Leifeng Pagoda, declaring the collapse as a major blow to the feudalistic social order that had ruled China for thousands of years. The essay was later included in a textbook for Chinese students and is well known throughout China.

Chinese experts long debated whether or not the Leifeng Pagoda should be rebuilt. A strong argument for the pagoda's rebuilding was that it had great archaeological value and was also an ancient architectural masterpiece. It also bore great potential as a major tourist attraction. In March of 2000, the restoration of Leifeng Pagoda officially began. A team of archaeologists went to the site of the Pagoda ruins and started the process of unearthing and discovering. A modern, seven-story structure was completed in 2002, accessed via escalator and elevator. It features archaeological exhibits and dedications on each floor with themes such as the Legend of the White Snake, examples of famous calligraphic writings, Wuyue period events associated with the Pagoda's construction, and a top floor dedicated to scenes from the life of the Buddha. The association of the Pagoda with the romantic story of the White Snake, coupled with its cultural heritage and commanding views over West Lake, make it the most popular tourist attraction in Hangzhou. A museum housing cultural artifacts, including two Aśoka-style stūpas minted by King Qian Chu as part of his dispersion of the Buddha's remains, is situated at some distance off to the side of the main Pagoda. It is but rarely visited in comparison.

The other monument in Hangzhou that I would like to discuss is the stūpa containing the relics of Yongming Yanshou (904–975). The Yongming Stūpa Hall is located in a private area off of Jingci (Pure mercy) Monastery, inaccessible to those who are unaware of its existence. Yanshou was a prominent Buddhist figure and associate of King Qian Chu, who played an important role as the leading spokesperson for Buddhism in the Wuyue kingdom. In 960, he was appointed by King Qian Chu as abbot of the newly constructed Yongming Monastery, which became the leading monastery in the Wuyue kingdom, a de facto headquarters where the official Buddhist teaching of the kingdom was disseminated. Because of the eclectic nature of his teaching, Yanshou enjoyed an evolving legacy in the Buddhist community, as promoter of blessings, patriarch in the Chan School, and Pure Land School patriarch. Eventually, Yanshou was regarded as a bodhisattva-like figure, receiver of petitions from those seeking rebirth in the Pure Land, and even as an incarnation of Amitabha Buddha, believed to preside over the Pure Land of the West in Buddhist cosmology. A special hall was constructed to house the Yongming Stūpa, which served as a focal point for the formation of a cult of worshippers dedicated to seeking Pure Land via petitions for Yanshou's assistance.[2] Like most Buddhist monuments, the Yongming Stūpa was destroyed during the Cultural Revolution and was rebuilt in the 1990s. The Hall that houses it was constructed in the Republican Period (1912–1949) (see figure 4.4). It has reemerged as a central focus for a Yanshou cult

Figure 4.4. Yanshou Stūpa, Hangzhou, China, with circumambulating worshippers. Photo by author.

with a membership of roughly one thousand, around fifty or so who take turns chanting while circumambulating the stūpas daily.

How do these two stūpas reflect the contemporary revival of Buddhism in China? The fact that their origins date from the same period over a thousand years ago, and that both were reconstructed and revived around the same time roughly twenty-five years ago, make them good sites for comparison. When we look at these two examples, they appear as the two poles regarding religious responses to "the complex of modernity" in contemporary China (discussed in the next section): conservative versus progressive.

The Yongming Stūpa, private and secluded, represents the response of the Buddhist faithful who wish to preserve the traditions of the past and ensure their continuation in the future. The fact that the Yongming Stūpa cult reconstituted itself after decades of nonactivity is a testament to the strength and dedication of devout Buddhist believers. The site itself is controlled and managed by the Buddhist establishment, under the auspices of (in descending order) the Hangzhou Buddhist Association, Jingci Temple, and the Yongming Stūpa Worship Society, with ultimate oversight by the Chinese Buddhist Association and CCP. The congregation of patrons who participate in cult activities at the site is elderly and largely female. They represent a model of Buddhist revival predicated on reconstructing the past.

Leifeng Pagoda represents a radically different model of "Buddhist" revival in contemporary China. While Leifeng Pagoda's origins are unequivocally tied to Buddhism, the history of the site and its associations with popular culture dilute its Buddhist heritage. The tussle between Buddhist sanctuary and tourist destination that the site represents falls heavily in favor of tourism and commercial interests. Even though Buddhism is acknowledged at the site, especially in its top-floor display and an affiliated museum, the masses of people who visit show little interest in Leifeng Pagoda as a Buddhist site. Displays of Buddhist piety are neither encouraged nor evident. In Leifeng Pagoda's case, the Buddhist revival, if it can even be said to be Buddhist, is predicated on contemporary realities that have little to do with Buddhism as a religion.

The Leifeng Pagoda model is quite complicated owing to various stakeholders with multiple interests. Figure 4.5 (on the next page) represents the variety of parties interested in Leifeng Pagoda.[3]

Diverse stakeholders promoted Leifeng Pagoda's revival and are vested in its prosperity. These include government executives in the

90 | The Future of China's Past

Figure 4.5. Leifeng Pagoda stakeholders. Author provided.

Hangzhou municipal government for whom the West Lake Scenic Area and Leifeng Cultural Park are pivotal tourist destinations. Admission to the park alone is a considerable source of revenue for municipal government coffers. As a cultural site, the Zhejiang Archaeological Association played a leading role in excavating and managing the development of the site, including the services of architects and artisans for erecting the new pagoda and creating the displays contained within it. Taken it its entirety, the project may be considered as part of a plan for economic growth based on heritage management and is an example of the kind of project one sees with regularity in local areas and municipalities throughout China as its economy moves from a production to a consumer-based model. The promotion of local heritage, as a result, is not driven by historical, cultural, or religious motivations but uses these in the service of stimulating economic activity, investment opportunity, and the growth of private ancillary businesses (e.g., the hospitality industry). These, in turn, provide employment opportunities to the local community. The community of Buddhist believers, not an inconsiderable group in a region like Hangzhou, also derives benefits from the celebration of their heritage and in some cases, like the Yongming Stūpa, actual access to sites important to their ritual activities. Even though Leifeng Pagoda provides no opportunities for ritual activities to members of the Buddhist community, it does increase general awareness and appreciation of the Buddhist contributions to Hangzhou culture.

While the two cases introduced here, Yongming Stūpa and the Leifeng Stūpa and Pagoda represent extremes, they are indicative of forces driving the Buddhist revival in China. Most sites fall somewhere in the middle. Lingyin (often translated literally as "Soul's Retreat") Monastery is also a major tourist draw and Buddhist pilgrimage site in the West Lake area and sits within a cultural park managed by the Hangzhou municipal government. There is no access to the monastery except through the park, which also contains the famous Buddhist grottoes of Feilaifeng (The peak that came flying [in from India]), situated adjacent to Lingyin Monastery. Entrance to the monastery requires separate admission. The number of pilgrims/tourists averages ten thousand per day. With the admission fee set at 30 CNY (roughly US$5), the revenue adds up quickly, totaling roughly 9 million CNY (1.3 million USD) per month, or 110 million CNY (nearly 16 million USD) per year on admissions alone. The entrance fee to the park itself is even higher, with full fare at double the rate (60 CNY) for the monastery, so the Hangzhou city government is also reaping rich rewards. Once inside the monastery, pilgrims/tourists are treated to periodic rituals performed by a fully functioning Buddhist institution, with chanting processions accompanied by musical chimes and drums performed by the roughly 130 resident monks. Observation reveals a mix of devout and casual Buddhists who take advantage of opportunities to make monetary and/or incense offerings and perform prostrations before Buddhist images. Especially devout laity (again, mostly women but not exclusively so) may be invited to join in chanting rituals especially designed for them by the monastery. Despite these opportunities, one gets the impression that most visitors are casual tourists who visit for reasons other than to express their Buddhist faith (e.g., to spend a leisurely outing with family or friends in a culturally enriching environment). There are lots of interesting things to see: monks in regalia performing ceremonies, colorful halls adorned with Buddhist deities and banners, altars decked out with paraphernalia to augment the grandeur of the deities worshipped, ancient historical monuments like two twin sets of towering stone-pagoda stūpas, one dating from King Qian Chu's reign in the Wuyue period in the tenth century, the other from the early eleventh century, a Five Hundred Arhats Hall, an alcove dedicated to Chan patriarchs, a hall housing the four Buddhist guardian deities, a Śākyamuni hall, a hall for the Medicine Buddha, a Budai (Cloth sack) Maitreya hall, a museum displaying heritage objects related to history of the monastery, a library, several gift shops, tea and coffee shops (even serving lattes), and so on. All in all, an argument can be made that the commercial aspects of the monastery sit comfortably with its religious functions and that the two are complementary.

Another pertinent example emblematic of the contemporary Buddhist revival in China is the Xuedou (Snowy Springs) Monastery in the Ningbo region. It was founded in the Tang dynasty (although legend claims it was founded before that, to the Jin dynasty, 265–420 CE) and like many famous Buddhist cultural sites in the region, it has an illustrious history. A few years ago, it won a province-wide competition to build a new Buddhist Academy for Zhejiang Province, a Buddhist college for training clergy. The college is located just outside the city of Xikou, famous as the hometown and former residence of Kuo-min tang (Guomindang) leader Chiang Kai-shek. The monastery complex is located a few kilometers away, up Xuedou Mountain from which it takes its name. Xuedou Monastery is an impressive complex with an array of buildings, features, and functions, similar to Lingyin Monastery and other major Buddhist monasteries in China. What distinguishes Xuedou is a rather peculiar dual-axis model. The majority of Buddhist monasteries in China are situated along a central axis, with the entrance and main worship halls situated on a central corridor. There may be and inevitably are side corridors, especially in the case of large complexes, adjacent to the central corridor on both sides (typically one side is devoted to the "business-side" of running the monastery and dealing with the outside world, while the other "religious-side" is for residing monks or nuns). Xuedou has, in effect, two central axes situated side by side, each with adjacent corridors. One of the axis is for the long-established monastery that houses its retinue of mostly monks (and some nuns) and carries out the traditional ritual and ceremonial functions of the monastery. The other axis is newly built. The crowning image, a stunning fifty-six-meter-high, golden-colored Great Maitreya statue (in the style of Budai Maitreya) situated on a hilltop overlooking and completing the axis, was dedicated in 2008. The final stages of building to complete the complex have been ongoing, As of May 2019, the final buildings were being erected. Although ritual functions are carried out at the new axis, its main function is as a showcase for a vision of Chinese Buddhism constructed to appeal to modern audiences. Feeling like a tourist theme park more than a monastery, it manages to walk visitors through a panoply of Buddhist history and culture amid the backdrop of the stunning scenery of the Xuedou Mountains. The journey up the axis culminates with an elevator ride up to the platform holding the Great Maitreya statue on the side of the hill (see figure 4.6). Photo

Figure 4.6. Budai Maitreya statue at Xuedou Monastery in Ningbo. Photo by author.

opportunities abound throughout the experience, especially from the Great Maitreya statue, or against it as a background.

The choice of Maitreya as the featured image of Xuedou is not accidental but is a result of strong ties between Maitreya and the region. In Buddhist lore, Maitreya is the future Buddha designated to usher in an era of peace and righteousness in line with Buddhist teachings and principles. According to Chinese tradition, Maitreya appeared over a thousand years ago in nearby Fenghua in the guise of an unkempt, disheveled monk. He became known as Budai (Cloth sack) Maitreya for the cloth sack he carried from a pole on his back containing his possessions as he wandered aimlessly without a permanent abode. Unlike the serious demeanor of other Buddhist figures, Budai Maitreya is distinguished by his jolly nature, humorous personality, and eccentric lifestyle. He is usually shown laughing or smiling, earning him the sobriquet "Laughing Buddha." He is also depicted as plump and well fed, earning him the nickname "Fat Buddha." While Maitreya's associations with the region make him a likely candidate for Xuedou to honor as a reigning Buddhist divinity, the designation is part of something more: a campaign to rebrand Xuedou as a fifth Buddhist sacred mountain in China. By tradition, China has four sacred Buddhist mountains: Mt. Wutai in Shanxi province, dedicated to Mañjuśri (C. Wenshu), the bodhisattva of wisdom; Mt. Emei in Sichuan province, dedicated to the bodhisattva Samantabadhra (C. Puxian), known for his strenuous practice; Mt. Jiuhua in Anhui province, dedicated to Ksitigarbha (C. Dizang), bodhisattva-protector of being in hell; and Mt. Putuo on an island in Zhejiang province, dedicated to Avalokitesvara (C. Guanyin), bodhisattva of compassion. The rebranding of Xuedou as China's fifth sacred Buddhist mountain puts it on the Chinese Buddhist map as a major tourist and pilgrimage site. While the association of the region with Maitreya has long been acknowledged and is a natural point of identification, the current rebranding effort has been spearheaded by local and provincial authorities who have invested large sums of money into the construction project on Xuedou (not to mention the resources committed to construct the new Buddhist Academy) in an effort to bring prominence to the region and make it an attractive destination.

Xi Jinping served as governor of Zhejiang province in 2002–2007, a period when many of the plans for Buddhist revival in the region took shape, especially at Xuedou and elsewhere in Ningbo. Xi is often pictured visiting monasteries in the area during his tenure as governor, and it is a point of pride (also implying official authorization) for the Buddhist establishments that display them. This suggests the strong role played by local and provincial governments (with approval at the national level) in the Buddhist revival, who see broad-ranging cultural and economic benefits stemming from their investments.

The Future of China's Buddhist Past

My comments in this chapter are restricted to the Buddhist revival in the capital Hangzhou and Zhejiang province. Zhejiang province, and southeastern China more generally, are traditional strongholds of Buddhism, and the strength of the revival there is understandable given the history of the region. Not all regions in China have such a rich history, but those that do have experienced a more or less comparable level of resurgence. What does this resurgence bode for China's Buddhist future?

Calculating the number of Buddhists in China is fraught with difficulty. Who should count? What level of commitment is required? Should the number include casual tourists who visit Buddhist sites as sightseers, perhaps with little knowledge or interest in Buddhism? According to the Pew Research Center demographic study on the Global Religious Landscape, "Religion & Public Life" (based on analysis of more than twenty-five hundred censuses, surveys, and population registers), 18.2 percent of China's population, or just over 244 million, qualify as Buddhists.[4] While a minority of China's population identifies as Buddhist, according to Pew, half of the world's population of 487.5 million Buddhists are Chinese. The next most populous Buddhist country is Thailand at 93.2 percent, accounting for over sixty-four million, just over a quarter of China in total numbers. These are remarkable statistics that underscore the importance and potential of Chinese Buddhism to the contemporary world.

If touristic Buddhism can be counted as "religious," Buddhism in China has a bright future. Buddhist institutions in China have become financially wealthy based on the success of the tourism model. This is attributable to rising wealth and the growth of a middle class, which in turn has presented opportunities for increased leisure activity. Capitalizing on the heritage sites either associated with Buddhism or under direct Buddhist control, the Chinese populace has had increased exposure to Buddhism and Buddhist values. The wealth accumulated by Buddhist institutions has been reinvested to further promote Buddhist activities.

The plans for a massive Buddhist Culture Center in Hangzhou, scheduled to open in the near future to showcase and promote the positive attributes of Buddhism, are a result of this success. On the other hand, the accumulation of wealth can lead to problems—charges of corruption and displays of opulence that many see as contrary to Buddhist values. While the circumstances surrounding the impulses to corruption may be modern in nature, Buddhist institutions in China have always been susceptible to such charges whenever they have encountered temptations that accompany financial success. Indeed, one of the hallmarks of Chinese Buddhism can be said to be its ability to accommodate and complement the pressures of secularization, to turn secular associations, whether with government officials or the business elite, into occasions for supporting and enhancing the Buddha dharma.

One reason for a rise in interest in Buddhism in China has been the result of a moral vacuum with the decline of CCP Marxist ideology. Xi Jinping's recent initiatives to increase CCP morale have often been couched in support for China's ideological heritage, especially Confucianism and Buddhism, which he sees as compatible with the Marxism-with-Chinese-characteristics approach that has defined Communism in China since the reforms of Deng Xiaoping. Yet it is clear that not all forms of religion, including Buddhism, are to be tolerated. In line with Xi and CCP policies, Buddhist leaders in China often speak publicly about Buddhist culture rather than Buddhist religion. Buddhism, as with other religions, is supported by the government to the extent that it serves the causes of the state. As an aspect of China's unique cultural heritage, Buddhist institutions represent a source of pride that contributes to national and social well-being. This preference for Buddhism as a cultural rather than a religious force is also evident in the way Buddhism is studied academically in China. Although the situation is changing somewhat, the discipline of religious studies is poorly represented at Chinese universities. Buddhism in China is typically studied as an aspect of philosophy, literature, or ancient textual studies. Where units devoted to Buddhism exist, they are usually subfields of these disciplines. This coincides with the CCP's preference for philosophy over religion as an academic category, where credibility is assigned first and foremost to traditions that can be counted as philosophies, and only secondarily to those regarded as religions. Movements based on what the CCP labels as superstitions (such as the spiritual practice known as Falun Gong) are regarded as subversive by the state, anathema to socialist values, and actively suppressed.

It is useful to keep in mind how the CCP administers policies on religion, including Buddhism according to three categories. Fenggang Yang, founding director of the Center on Religion and Chinese Society at Purdue University, posits a three-fold categorization (what Yang calls "markets") for religious expression in China, designated as red, gray, and black.[5]

- Red practices are officially authorized by CCP as enhancing socialist values.

- Gray practices are tolerated, but not officially recognized and vulnerable to persecution.

- Black practices are officially proscribed by CCP as superstitions and counter to socialist values.

Red, gray, and black designations do not apply to individual religions per se but to aspects within individual traditions. In other words, there is "red" Buddhism, officially authorized by the CCP as enhancing socialist values; "gray" Buddhism, tolerated, but not officially recognized and vulnerable to persecution at the whim of the government; and "black" Buddhism, officially proscribed by the CCP as superstition and counter to socialist values. The same distinctions hold true for the other officially recognized religions in China: Daoism, Islam, Protestantism, and Catholicism.

Yang's characterization as applied to contemporary Buddhism shares general similarities with its premodern counterpart. Some years ago, the French Sinologist Jacques Gernet outlined a model for how Buddhism functioned in Chinese society based on material and economic criteria. While noting the great diversity that characterizes the Buddhist institutional presence in China, from great monasteries housing dozens of monks to village chapels and mountain hermitages with one or two inhabitants, Gernet also called attention to a similar diversity in terms of status:

> Some monasteries are official places of worship and are recognized as such. They have received their name (*e*) by imperial bestowal as well as gifts of land, funds, servants, allotments of local families, and certain privileges. They are entitled to annual subventions from the court. Their monks have been selected and ordained by the emperor

and are supervised by officially appointed clergy who are held accountable for their conduct. The other kind[s] of establishments are merely tolerated and are always the first to fall victim to repressions. These are private places of worship, serving the great families as well as the people.[6]

Following the distinction in status accorded Buddhist institutions, Gernet stipulates that there were three kinds of Chinese monks: "the official monk, maintained at state expense and responsible for the performance of ceremonies of the imperial cult"; "the private monk, fed and clothed by the great families"; and "the common monk who lived in the countryside, either in isolation or as a member of a small group." Great divides of privilege and power separated these three types of institutions and the monks who inhabited them.

In terms of the CCP's use of Buddhism as a tool of foreign policy, one can point to the World Buddhist Forums, the first of which was held in Hangzhou and Zhoushan (Zhejiang), which includes the location of the famous Buddhist mountain on Putuo Island, in 2006. This was the first major international religious conference held since the founding of the People's Republic in 1949. Subsequent Forums have been regularly held in Wuxi (Jiangsu), Hong Kong, and Putian (Fujian). The administration of Buddhism in China, including the sponsorship of these World Buddhist Forums, is done through the Buddhist Association of China. Since 2018 the Buddhist Association of China has been overseen by the United Front Work Department, a department that reports directly to the Central Committee of the CCP, when the State Administration of Religious Affairs was absorbed into it.

Buddhist "soft power" has also been utilized by the CCP in international arenas. In addition to the more well-known material dimensions of China's Belt and Road Initiative (BRI) in Southeast Asia through multibillion-dollar investments in transport infrastructure and industrial sites, the CCP has sought to build influence at the ideational level through the use of Buddhism as a cultural resource.[7] Since the advent of BRI in 2013, there has been a surge in outreach orchestrated through the offices of the United Front Work Department to Southeast Asia's Buddhist leaders and communities in Thailand, Myanmar, Cambodia, and Laos. These outreach efforts are being used to promote China's political goals, even though they are sanctioned by a party that remains staunchly atheist. China's use of Buddhism as an adjunct to the BRI in mainland

Southeast Asia suggests it is seeking to inspire a sense of shared values and to quiet any criticism about undue Chinese influence associated with BRI in Southeast Asian states.

In addition, numerous Buddhist academies have been established (or reestablished) throughout China in recent decades. The purpose of these academies is to provide core training for the Buddhist clergy and to educate them in both their duties to their religion and to the state. The Hangzhou Buddhist Academy, for example, claims to have trained "a number of modern monks who are patriotic, . . . have a high sense of historical mission and social responsibility, and can adapt to the trend of globalization and diversified development."[8] Monks trained at the academy pursue a number of subjects pertaining to the history of Buddhism, especially the doctrines and practices of the various schools of Chinese Buddhism but also auxiliary courses in subjects such as Chinese and Western philosophy, general psychology, sociology of religion, formal logic, the history of science and technology, and English.

If anything, the CCP has probably done a more thorough job supervising Buddhism than governments in the past. One senses far fewer instances of unauthorized religious expression in the case of Chinese (Han) Buddhism. The situation becomes more complex, however, when we look at CCP policy in terms of Tibetan Buddhism, where the government maintains vigilance over unauthorized practices. This is also true of Christianity, especially the phenomenon of "house" (or private) churches that operate outside the purview of CCP oversight. The same holds for certain forms of Islam, especially on government suspicion when Islamic ideas are linked with independence sentiments, as in Xinjiang.

Chapter Five

Back to the Future?

Prospects for Confucianism and Chinese Traditions in Contemporary China

Why Focus on Confucianism?

As explored in chapter 2, the revival of Confucianism in China is among the most unprecedented events in modern Chinese history. Given the antipathy toward Confucius in CCP rhetoric and the anti-Confucian policies in the early decades of PRC rule, the rise of Confucius may be likened to rising from the dead. The role of Confucianism in Chinese culture had long been a topic of conversation in the modern period, dating from the years of Qing dynasty decline and its eventual fall in 1912. With the advent of Communist rule in China, interest in Confucianism completely dissipated. Confucius was cast as the greatest of Chinese villains, as the one who instigated cultural modes that kept China weak in the face of Western domination and subjugated the people by sanctioning a landlord class that exploited the peasantry. These themes resonated with New Culture movement themes and Marxist rhetoric. Outside of mainland China interest in Confucianism continued in Chinese diasporic and international communities who saw in Confucianism either continuity with local traditions or a historical artifact of a vibrant and vital premodern tradition. Few suggested that Confucianism continued to have much in the way of contemporary relevance. While diasporic and international forces can be credited with keeping Confucianism alive (or at least on life support), the reversal of fortunes for Confucianism has gained significant momentum with Xi Jinping's pro-Confucian rhetoric in recent years. The unprecedented support from the CCP leader and his association of Confucian values with CCP values have resulted in discussions among Chinese Confucians regarding the revival of Confucianism and its renewed importance and relevance.

The current chapter explores some key questions for the contemporary Confucian agenda as it attempts to reformulate itself for the twenty-first century. I focus on Confucianism given the dominant role it has played in China's past. Of all China's traditions, it is the one most likely to assume a leading role in China's future. Among the basic questions are those about Confucianism itself: What is it? What does it constitute? And what does it mean to be Confucian? Added to these questions of basic identity, there are twenty-first-century concerns that impede a Confucian reformulation. These stem from societal foundations formulated on vastly different principles and value structures than those of the East Asian past when Confucianism thrived. How, for example, does a twenty-first-century Confucian respond to concerns emanating from liberal democracies with their concerns for individual rights and protections, gender rights, equality, and so on? How are Confucianism and Communism compatible? My investigation begins with an exploration of these challenges against the backdrop of the past, particularly in conversation with the Neo-Confucian reinvention of the tradition from the Song dynasty onward. In chapter 1, I discussed the three critical periods in Chinese history recognized not only for their evolution of existing patterns but also as ground-breaking paradigm shifts that break with the old and usher in the new. Up until the early twentieth century, two such periods are recognized: the end of the Warring States period and the advent of the Qin and Han dynasties in the third century BCE, and the fall of the Tang and advent of the Song dynasty in the tenth century CE. The paradigm initiated in the Song lasted through the Qing dynasty. Central to this reinvention was a complex interrelationship of Confucianism with ideas emanating from Chinese Buddhism and Daoism. Historically, Confucianism borrowed extensively from these traditions while charting new courses for revival—remaining true to its foundations while accommodating disparate and seemingly contradictory elements. This history of borrowing may serve as a model for Confucians to contemplate as they confront twenty-first-century realities, the so-called third iteration of the Confucian tradition. Admittedly, this is a very Confucian view of Chinese history, but it weighs heavily on modern and contemporary efforts by Confucians to initiate a new Confucian renaissance of Chinese culture and civilization.

The Song Dynasty, the Genesis of Neo-Confucianism (the Second Iteration), and Its Meaning for Contemporary New Confucianism (the Third Iteration)

The early Song dynasty is commonly acknowledged as one of the great turning points of Chinese (if not world) history. In the 1930s, Naitō Konan, Japanese historian, Sinologist, and founder of the Kyoto School of historiography, famously labeled the Tang-Song transition as an important watershed from "medieval" (*chūsei*) to "early modern" (*kinsei*) periods. Buried within the seamless template of this historical transition was a furtive debate over the nature of China's culture—what constituted it, how it should be defined, and what should be included. The early Song rulers, Taizu (r. 960–976), Taizong (r. 976–997), and Zhenzong (r. 997–1022) succeeded where predecessors had failed in turning the page on the century-old period of chaos that preceded them, advocating a culture of *wen* (or literary culture) as opposed to *wu* (martial prowess). This turning point heralded a revival of interest in China's past, initially coalescing in a movement known as *Song xue*, or "Song Learning," a broad-based exploration of antiquity and the more recent past in the hopes of reconstituting lost *wen* resources. This earlier phase was eventually supplanted by a need to define *wen* more systematically and comprehensively: although to be fair, this concern had persisted in literary circles since Han Yu's famous diatribe against Buddhist influences on Chinese culture in the late Tang. The retrospective view of the Song dynasty as the "age of Confucianism," exhibited in works like the *History of the Song* (*Song shi*), is but a teleological tribute culminating in the great thinker Zhu Xi's formulation of a newly ascendant Neo-Confucian orthodoxy. The reality was much more complicated, and the debates of the early Song period may be likened to a second "hundred schools of thought," the furtive debates about the nature of China's culture in the Zhou dynasty. I draw from my research to characterize the dynamics of debate over *wen* in the early Song period. The following table reduces representative perspectives in the early Song dynasty to six groups.[1] Rather than speak of "Confucians" during this period, it is preferable to use the more general Chinese word, *Ru*. In many cases, the term *Ru* is synonymous with Confucian, but it also allows for wider inclusion of those from other traditions who belong to the *Ru* tradition of literati or *belletrists*—connoisseurs of fine writing. It is this more inclusive sense that fits the early Song dynasty context (and many contexts in Chinese history), where *Ru* were not only Confucians, strictly speaking, but also Buddhists with Confucian leanings, Confucians with Buddhist leanings, and other literati who sought expressions of *wen* who were not limited by restrictive Confucian definitions. Table 5.1 surveys the gamut of responses that the search for a new paradigm in late tenth- and early eleventh-century China produced.

Space does not allow me to discuss this table in detail but to note the existence of multiple types of *Ru*, or literati advocates of harder and softer interpretations of *guwen*, the classical prose movement that advocated clarity and precision in written expression, a return to the classical period of early Confucian writing, as opposed to the ornate style that had risen in its wake. A group of *Ru* Buddhists emerged, advocating Confucianism as a basis for China's *wen* culture, augmented by Buddhist teachings. They were admired more for their skill in literary (*wen*) arts than their expertise in Buddhist doctrine (although they were proficient in that as well). Daoists are missing from the table, since they did not emerge as a powerful influence upon court circles until later in the dynasty.

Doctrinal Buddhist literati espoused traditional Buddhist literary styles and were known as traditional advocates of Buddhist teachings. Secular and Buddhist literati exponents of Linji Chan advocated spontaneity and freedom of expression, highly prized in certain court circles as an innovative

Table 5.1. Responses to Creating Cultural (*Wen*) Models in the Early Song Dynasty

Group 1	Group 2	Group 3	Group 4	Group 5	Group 6
Intolerant *guwen* 不寬容古文	Tolerant *guwen* 寬容古文	*Ru* Buddhists 儒僧	Doctrinal Buddhists 教理僧	Chan Literati 禪文人	Linji Chan 臨濟禪
(Han Yu)/ 韓愈 Liu Kai/ 柳開	Wang Yucheng/ 王禹偁 Xu Xuan/ 徐鉉	Zanning/ 贊寧 Zhiyuan/ 智圓	Yanshou/ 延壽 Shengchang/ 省常 Zhili/ 知禮	Yang Yi/ 楊億 Li Zunxu/ 李遵勗	(Yixuan)/ 義玄 Shengnian/ 省念

type of *wen* that distinguished the Song dynasty from the Tang and previous dynasties. The spectrum suggests that definitions of *wen* were fluid, and the *Ru* who espoused them represented a broad range of perspectives.

This tolerance for differing perspectives did not last. While the Song *wen* movements remained more fluid than Confucian retellings would have us believe, the *guwen* perspective eventually came to dominate. It centered around an exclusive commitment to Confucian sources and the moral principles espoused in them, with a lesser degree of tolerance toward other traditions. Buddhism and Daoism were officially sidelined and would struggle to retain minority status in succeeding dynasties. Yet the narrative of Neo-Confucian ascendancy is only partially accounted for in this retelling. Even a glancing comparison between classical Confucianism and Neo-Confucianism reveals the tremendous transformation that occurred as a result of Buddhist and Daoist influences. To put it briefly, Buddhism (and to a lesser extent Daoism) supplied the questions, to which Confucianism provided new answers. The Buddhist agenda is apparent, for example, in the Neo-Confucian preoccupation with such things as mind (*xin*), nature (*xing*), and principle (*li*). The Neo-Confucian form of meditation, *jingzuo*, or "quiet sitting," as a technique for spiritual cultivation is but a Confucian repurposing of Buddhist *zuochan*, "sitting meditation." Neo-Confucian metaphysics and psychology are but a calculated response to Buddhism, with notable influences from Daoism, especially in the development of New-Confucian metaphysics. Early or "classical" Confucianism had little to say on such matters. Whatever sources existed in the earlier Confucian tradition were recast on a cosmological scale influenced by Buddhist theories. In addition, the very basis for the study of Confucianism was reformed in conjunction with evolving Buddhist preferences. The Neo-Confucian transition from the Five Classics to the Four Books parallels the Buddhist shift from classical scriptural sources, the sūtras and their commentaries, to *yulu*, or dialogue records, of contemporary Chan masters. The preference for a direct communication style, pithy and to the point, over tedious commentary fueled an exegetical revolution that cut across ideological preferences. Finally, Zhu Xi's twelfth-century invectives against the lack of moral grounding in Buddhism mimic the late Tang Buddhist-literatus Zongmi's argument for a morally grounded Buddhism versus the iconoclastic and ethically suspect antics of the Hongzhou Chan school.[2]

My point is not to brand Neo-Confucianism as unoriginal but, to the contrary, to suggest that its success was predicated on the creative responses it made to the challenges presented by the new Buddhist agendas. Neo-Confucian success was ultimately attributable to an ability to adapt core Confucian orientations and moral principles to unforeseen, unimagined agendas. This is the lesson from the past that the Confucian legacy bears as Confucians confront the current situation and attempt to redeem their tradition in a third, modern iteration.

Confucianism and the "Complex of Modernity"

The "complex of modernity" is a major paradigm in the social sciences stemming from the rise of the West and its global impact. As Steven Seidman comments, "Modern social theory crystallized as an effort to explain but also justify or shape the emerging cultural complex of modernity."[3] This cultural complex has many far-reaching tentacles, too numerous to enumerate here; suffice it to say, it is the root system of our modern world. As framed by Stefano Varese, "Contemporary science and knowledge (thus theory of knowledge and epistemology) are integral parts of the socio-ideological complex of modernity-colonialism-capitalism."[4] Among the tentacles that support the "complex of modernity," the one I would like to focus on here, is morality. Niccolò Machiavelli is widely credited with the turn away from "conventional moral and religious standards of human conduct" toward "a vision of political rule purged of extraneous moralizing influences."[5] This turn away from moral behavior as the template for proper conduct seems to me to be an aspect of the cultural complex of modernity that a revived *Ruism* must confront.

Along with the modern turn away from moral behavior as a fundamental basis for evaluating human character, the authorization of the individual as active agent and source of authority is another aspect of the cultural complex of modernity that poses problems for New Confucians. While it is relatively easy for modern Confucians to fault individualism for its excesses and the democratic rights and privileges that accompany it, how might they position themselves to confront the hegemonic behemoth, the cultural complex of modernity itself? Take, for example, a comment by Singapore's former prime minister Lee Kuan Yew, that Asians have "little doubt that a society with communitarian values where the interests of society take precedence over that of the individual suits them better than the individualism of America."[6] Even as Chinese officials protest the hegemony of human rights,[7] a cogent program to replace such fundamental mechanisms that have girded the international order will need to be conceived and implemented to persuade others to participate in and support.

A Prospectus of Confucian Models and Agendas for the Twenty-First Century

The emergence of China as a major force in international affairs, both economically and politically, poses serious challenges to the hegemony of Western liberal democratic values, including the human rights regime implemented through the United Nations and other international bodies following the Second World War. This is the leading intellectual issue of the twenty-first century and will have significant implications for such diverse areas as diplomatic relations, international aid policies, domestic and international law, and more. In short, it offers the very real potential for an alternative hegemonic regime based on non-Western liberal democratic values: the most significant departure in international affairs since the fall of the Soviet Union and the end of the Cold War.

The lessons from the past suggest that there are many ways to define *Ru* and that the construction of Ruism, itself, is rooted in a particular historical consciousness. One of the fundamental questions is how inclusive should *Ru* be. Is Ruism a synonym for Confucianism, and if so, what kind of Confucianism should Ruism embrace? My brief excursus into the Song dynasty earlier in this chapter suggests that the core curriculum for Ruism is rooted in Confucian texts, but even here, we must ask ourselves which ones. Confucian study today presumes the authority of the Four Books, the *Lunyu*, *Mengzi*, *Great Learning*, and *Doctrine of the Mean*, as if these represented the original Confucius message, from the mouths of the Confucian sages themselves. Few pause to reflect on the fact that this approach is the reconstructed agenda of Neo-Confucianism, that classical Confucianism was predicated on a study of the Five Classics, *Shujing* (Classic of [historical] documents), *Shijing* (Classic of poetry), *Liji* (Classic of ritual propriety), *Yijing* (Classic of changes), and *Chunqiu* (Spring and autumn annals). Regardless of which Confucian core is arrived at, the more important question seems to be: what kinds of materials might be allowed to augment that core? Traditional fundamentalists were intolerant and excluded all but the Confucian core. Not only were texts from other schools of thought ignored, but even Confucian-guided writings like the dynastic histories were excluded. With the Confucian sense of hierarchy, it seems that a graded system of inclusion, with Confucian classics at the center and others at the periphery on a graduated scale, would be possible. This, too, would allow for an expansive definition of *Ru* to include literary types of various persuasions. In the modern context, it would allow for expanding the network of sources beyond the Confucian and East Asian world to include world classics from other regions.

While important, mechanical questions around who and what are included do not address the central ideological issues that need to be confronted, namely the modern approach to "morality" (considered by many as immoral) and democratic-based individualism. The radical fundamentalist would eschew the modernist agenda and advocate for a return to morality and communitarian values (Confucian based). Here, I agree with Sam Crane that "while it may be true that certain individuals will find the commitment and fortitude to enact duty according to ritual and progress toward humanity in a manner consistent with Confucius's thought, not enough individuals will do so to justify defining China as a "Confucian" society. The tension between Confucian morality and modern life is just too great." And if the burden of reviving Confucianism is too much for ordinary Chinese to endure, how attractive will it be for non-Chinese? And, as Crane and others have suggested, Xi Jinping's turn to Confucianism is somewhat disingenuous, a ploy by an authoritarian regime to harness the excesses of corruption that threaten the legitimacy of the ruling party.[8] In one sense, Xi may be likened to a lot of his imperial predecessors who hide behind Confucianism to legitimize a Legalist authoritarian regime. While Xi's use of Confucianism is rooted in a particular milieu, it points to a larger question. In a modern context, can Confucianism escape being merely a tool in the service of others (in spite of the famous injunction attributed to Confucius in the *Lun yu*: "Don't be a tool")? Within the broader "complex of modernity" discourse, is Confucianism simply a communitarian card to be played to highlight the excesses of an entrenched individualism, or as it is used by Xi, to reinvigorate a moral consciousness among a corrupt leadership? If so, challenges to prevailing systems will be minimal, without substantial impact.

As Confucians contemplate a future for Confucianism, one may recall some of the lessons gained from the Neo-Confucian experience. Neo-Confucians remained true to a core set of moral principles and guidelines, while at the same time adapting and adopting new perspectives, concepts, and methods. It was the ability to adapt and adopt that proved successful. Not only was the new Confucianism a revival of old values but also an acquisition of new ones. The combination served as an alternative that attracted broad support. This, it seems, points to the possibility of a successful strategy moving forward. It is important to remember, as well, that the Neo-Confucian agenda was the result of a long process involving shedding an old skin and acquiring a new one, requiring the energy of many creative minds over hundreds of years. Still, at this writing, it is doubtful that people raised on the modern experience of relative freedom will be eager to embrace moral strictures that limit individual expression. This will seem nothing more than a return to an unenviable past, where moral choices were limited by a kind of priesthood, either religious or secular, rather than a way forward.

Whither Confucianism? The Two Roads of Contemporary Confucianism

In the introduction, I spoke of "The Fall and Rise of Confucius in Modern China." I now turn attention to some leading trends in the contemporary Confucian revival. Jiang Qing's recent essay, "From Mind Confucianism to Political Confucianism," offers a template for two alternative models that confront contemporary Confucianism.[9] The first, according to Jiang Qing, is "Mind Confucianism," referring to contemporary Neo-Confucianism as it has developed outside mainland China. It is an attempt to recast Confucianism in terms of modern Western political institutions of liberal democracy, based on a Confucian emphasis on "inner virtue" (moral idealism) as a complement to Western political institutions. The second is "Political Confucianism," which Jiang Qing casts as a return to authentic Confucianism, developed by him and others on the Chinese mainland. It advocates Confucian political development founded on the essentials of virtue-based Confucian values and posits a Confucian "external system" (social realism) as a complementary outgrowth of "inner virtue." Such a development would replace Western political institutions with a Confucian institutional system, to restore an authentic Confucianism based in "inner virtue" applied to an "external system."

Explained in more detail, contemporary Neo-Confucianism, known as "Mind Confucianism," refers in Chinese to *xinxing ruxue*, literally

"Mind-Nature Confucianism." Its main concern is the existential life of human individuals and their mental development, rather than sociopolitical institutions. It is based on religious resources drawn from the Confucian tradition, strongly emphasizing the issue of *neisheng*, namely, the development of individual morality and the self-cultivation of virtue within modern liberal democratic social-political institutions. It assumes the social-political system of liberal democracy. Absorbed by the existential realities of individuals' lives, "Mind Confucians" assume liberal democracy as the social-political system that Confucianism has to accept. They fail, according to Jiang Qing, to explore a type of politics (or "external system") that is authentic to traditional Confucianism and crucial for maintaining a civilized and orderly Confucian society within which its members can cultivate Confucian virtues. In Jiang Qing's view "Mind Confucians" have essentially individualized Confucianism, downplaying the relation-based, family-centered, and politics-relevant features of Confucianism. He asserts that this individualized Confucianism is contrary in spirit to actual Confucianism, as anyone who has read Confucius is aware of the nonindividualistic characteristics of Confucian thought that are embodied in fundamental Confucian concerns, including the Confucian use of rites (*li*) and music (*yue*) for virtue cultivation.

According to Jiang Qing, because contemporary Neo-Confucians regard liberal democracy as the ultimate standard for reconstructing Confucianism, they simply colonize Chinese culture with Western culture, altering the basic orientation of the Confucian spirit. Their mistakes, claim Jiang Qing, are twofold: (1) they draw exclusively on the resources of Mind Confucianism to develop Confucian politics, and (2) they borrow modern Western philosophy to recast the central concerns of Confucianism. What they neglect and ignore is the other significant strand of Confucianism: political Confucianism.

Political Confucianism is essentially a call to return to the original classical texts of Confucianism as understood through the original texts written or compiled by Confucius. Contrary to Mind Confucianism, Political Confucianism is mainly concerned with society and social relations rather than the spiritual life of individuals. Political Confucianism focuses on social-political reality rather than metaphysical and philosophical concepts and reasoning, which is the purview of Mind Confucianism. Political Confucianism, Jiang Qing contends, regards human nature as innately neither good nor bad based on empirical experience, unlike Mind Confucianism, which maintains an a priori assumption that human nature is innately good. By contrast, Political Confucianism holds that human beings are not born with a good nature but can become good if they are appropriately nurtured by their environment after birth. Broadly speaking, the contrast between Mind Confucianism and Political Confucianism articulated by Jiang Qing imitates the debate in Classical Confucianism between Mengzi (Mencius) and Xunzi, who similarly disagreed over whether human nature was innately good or not. Following Xunzi, Jiang Qing advocates a Political Confucianism that uses institutions to scrutinize and correct the dark side of human nature. Unlike Mind Confucianism, Political Confucianism does not assume there is an innate force within humans capable of correcting human nature. Rather, in order to counter and correct bad human behavior, it is necessary to rely on external forces such as sociopolitical institutions or a system of rites. Finally, it is important to note for Jiang Qing that although Political Confucianism has these merits, it is not opposed to Mind Confucianism. Rather, a complete account of Confucianism must achieve the appropriate unity of Political and Mind Confucianism.

Three Dimensions of Political Legitimacy in the Politics of the Kingly Way

One of the most intriguing applications of Jiang Qing's call to reestablish a political Confucianism and provide an "external structure" to complement its program of "internal virtue," thus mitigating any dependence on the sociopolitical structure of liberal democracy, is his proposal for the formation of a tri-cameral legislature. Jiang Qing's proposal is based on the Confucian vision of the Kingly Way (*wangdao*), a harmonization of the three dimensions that comprise the Chinese universe: Heaven, Human, and Earth. This is conveniently depicted in the Chinese language with the use of three horizontal lines 三, meaning "three," and one vertical line to form the character *wang* 王, meaning "king" or "ruler," implying that the ruler represents a human embodiment of the *axis mundi*, the point of connection between Heaven and Earth. The Heaven dimension implies a sanction by the holy and transcendent Dao (Heavenly way) as expressed or implied in Confucian scriptures and interpreted by prestigious Confucian scholars. The human dimension suggests there is no deviation from the mainstream of national cultural heritage nor any break with the historical continuity of nationality (i.e., ancestors). The earth dimension maintains compliance with the will or endorsement of the common people.

For Jiang Qing, this Confucian concept of *wangdao* may be developed into an "external structure" to support the maintenance of a Confucian social and political matrix, manifested as a tri-cameral legislature including a House of Profound Confucians, a House of National Continuity, and a House of Plebeians. The House of Profound Confucians represents the legitimacy of the sacred Way. The House of National Continuity represents the legitimacy of cultural heritage and tradition. The House of Plebeians represents the legitimacy of the common people's will and desire. The particular way in which the members of each house of the legislature are chosen and the mechanisms of checks and balances among the three houses are quite complex, according to Jiang Qing, and have yet to be fully elaborated. But he is able to provide a hint. The members of the House of Profound Confucians are to be chosen by nomination and appointment by nongovernmental Confucian organizations and official Confucian institutions. The members of the House of National Continuity should be representatives of religions (including Buddhism, Daoism, Islam, and Christianity) and the descendants of ancient sages and historical figures. The members of the Plebian House are to be chosen through elections and functional constituencies. According to Jiang's opinion in "An Explanation of the Diagram of the Kingly Way," the position of the House of Profound Confucians is the highest of the three houses, with the Plebeian House the lowest, and the House of National Continuity situated in between. Bills of great importance are to be passed simultaneously by all three, which become law. Those not reaching this mark are to be delayed, suspended, or vetoed. The hope is that the tri-cameral legislature will embody the theory of tri-dimensional legitimacy, an application of the Confucian principle of the Kingly Way.

Jiang Qing's proposal for a tri-cameral legislature is intriguing in many respects. First of all, the omission of a role for the Communist Party seems a fatal oversight, unless it is imagined for a Chinese future where the Party has relinquished power (a somewhat treasonous proposition). It is optimistic to suggest the ruling Communist Party, given their tenacious hold on power, would ever submit to such a proposal. Secondly, despite its presentation as a radical departure from Mind Confucianism's acceptance of and dependence on the liberal democratic political order, Jiang Qing's suggestion to admit a branch of legislature whose members are chosen by election and functional constituencies, the House of Plebeians, is a major compromise to the very liberalism he speaks out against. Mencius's acknowledgment of the "will of the people" as a major force in dynastic change, often materializing in the armed insurgencies of disenfranchised peasants, could be accommodated in Jiang Qing's third house. This institutionalization of a major source for potential discontent could go a long way in breaking the pattern of violence that accompanies political change in Chinese history. Thirdly, the constitution of and the roles assumed by the two upper houses, the House of Profound Confucians and the House of National Continuity, replicate the constitution of and roles played by similar parties in imperial China, where Confucians were granted privilege of place in court politics and administrative affairs, while Buddhist and Daoists were placed in marginal roles, if not completely ostracized. And to return to implications suggested in the first point, the Confucian elite in traditional China ruled at the behest of the emperor, not as an institution unto themselves. Their major tool was remonstration (i.e., persuasion) to influence the emperor to choose wisely (i.e., according to Confucian counsel) in implementing policies. In Jiang's proposal, there is no emperor, of course, and there is no indication that Jiang advocates returning to this aspect of the Confucian past, even though his invoking of the Kingly Way (*wangdao*), where the ruler represents a human embodiment of the *axis mundi*, is predicated on such a position.

The Future of China's Past: Confucianism, Legalism, Daoism, and Buddhism as Supports for the Ruler

Amplifying on Jiang Qing's suggestions, augmented by a historical precedent stemming from a suggestion put forth in the early Song dynasty drawn from my research, I would like to propose a possible model for cooperative harmony whereby China's resurgent traditions might buttress authoritarian rule in contemporary China. This is not my recommendation or prediction but rather my assessment of probabilities that could include provisional roles for China's traditions in a way forward in the immediate future. In many ways, Xi Jinping has already put in place the possibilities of positive roles for China's traditions in socialist China. Let's explore further how and why this might work.

I mentioned previously the significant situation that modern China has faced, constituting a third paradigm shift in China's long evolution as a culture. To repeat, the first major shift was the transition out of the Warring States period into imperial rule in the Qin and Han dynasties in the third century BCE. The second shift occurred with the decline and demise of the Tang dynasty, another Warring States–type interregnum, before the reunification of China in the Song dynasty in the tenth century CE. Confucianism buttressed by Legalism and other traditions, Daoism and Buddhism, provided the ideological and administrative framework for both of these iterations, retroactively referred to as Classical Confucianism and Neo-Confucianism. With the intrusion of Western imperialism into the region, the old Confucian paradigm was demolished by both external and internal forces. The victory of Communist forces in 1949 advanced a new paradigm for China based on Marxist ideology. The old traditions were cast as obstacles to China's modern progress and were presumed all but dead, anachronisms of a past age. With the death of Mao in 1976 and the passing of his influence over CCP policy, a new era of Communism in China emerged under the leadership of Deng Xiaoping. Deng's policies, under the rubric of "socialism with Chinese characteristics," were decidedly more open and tolerant. China began to progress economically, accompanied by a resurgence of China's traditional cultural institutions. The current CCP leader, Xi Jinping, officially branded as "leader for life," has further encouraged the development of China's traditions and their integration into CCP aims and policies. While recent signals suggest that Xi is reinvigorating Marxist ideology as the bulwark of Chinese ideology, the resurgence of Chinese traditions has some Confucian proponents eyeing a new "Chinese traditions (principally Confucianism) with socialist characteristics" framework.

My suggestion for how provisional roles for China's traditions might be included echoes my research into the early Song dynasty context. The table, "Responses to Creating Cultural (*Wen*) Models in the Early Song Dynasty," at the beginning of this chapter included a category (Group Three) for Buddhist *Ru*, Buddhists who embraced Confucianism and integrated it into their *wen* cultural program. A leading proponent of this group was the tenth-century Buddhist scholar-administrator, Zanning, who espoused a "grand strategy of the three teachings" as a way to embrace and validate each of China's three traditions—Confucianism, Daoism, and Buddhism.[10] In Zanning's proposal, each of the three traditions support the emperor and the imperial mission, forming a tripod-like structure propping up and assisting the emperor in conducting affairs of state. While Zanning's proposal appears to be a magnanimous Buddhist-inspired altruism, it was, in fact, a recognition that the Chinese cultural world had changed, that Buddhist ideological dominance could no longer be assumed, and that Buddhist survival depended on compromise and the acknowledgment that the way forward necessitated a new model. As described by Zanning, the "grand strategy of the three teachings" included the following propositions:

1. The emperor, as the undisputed head of the Chinese state and leader of Chinese society, is the legitimate supervisor of each of the three teachings (including the Buddhist religion);

2. Each teaching (including Buddhism) is useful to the emperor for conducting affairs of state;

3. Each of China's three teachings—Buddhism, Confucianism, and Daoism—have a legitimate position in the function of the state; and

4. It is the duty of the emperor to supervise the activities of the three teachings, and direct them in accordance with the aims of the state.

The suggestion is that if any leg of the tripod (any of the three teachings) is lacking, the vessel (the imperial dynasty) will collapse. For Zanning, this was graphically suggested by the bronze *ding* vessel, a three-legged structure used for offering sacrificial food (see figure 5.1 on next page). The fate of the empire depends on harmonious cooperation among the three teachings, with the emperor's oversight, encouragement, and support.

The fate of Zanning's "grand strategy" was less than hoped. As the reality of the Confucian revival took hold among the Song dynasty bureaucracy, the dependence of the imperial position on Confucian teaching became apparent. As the influence of Confucian teaching became pronounced, the tripod began to resemble more of a monopod, with nonessential supports (Daoism and Buddhism) consigned to peripheral and marginal roles. Yet, it is instructive to invoke Zanning's proposed model in the early Song dynasty to the situation at hand. How might Zanning's "grand strategy" be applied in Xi Jinping's China?

Instead of a support structure buttressing the authority of the state, Xi Jinping's China suggests a command structure of authority issued from the top (the reality of authoritarian models in premodern China as well). Figure 5.2 (on next page) shows the structure of authority in the CCP.

Figure 5.1. Ding vessel, Late Shang dynasty, Shanghai Museum. February 26, 2006. Public domain.

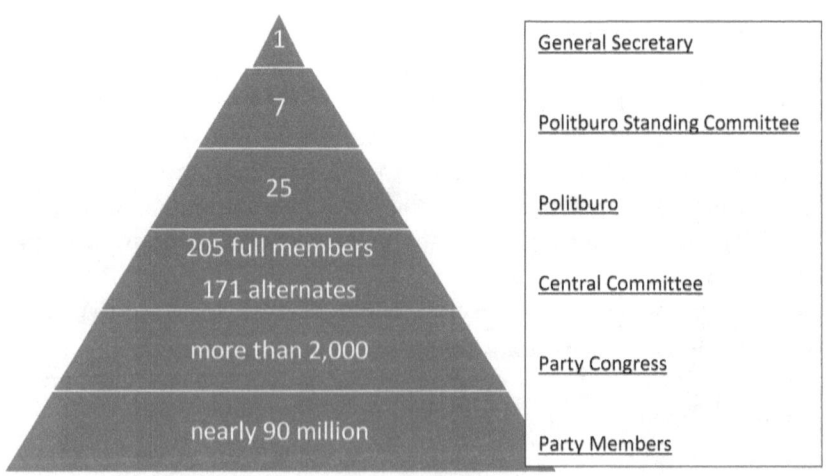

Figure 5.2. The Chinese Communist Party (after Jarrod Fankhauser, ABC News, posted March 5, 2019). Author provided.

The way the Communist Party incorporates traditions/religions in China is shown in figure 5.3. In this case, the authoritarian structure buttresses the socialist state of the CCP. This is represented by the two-thousand-plus-member Party Congress (selected from over ninety million Party members), the 205-member Central Committee, the twenty-five-member Politburo, the seven-member Politburo Standing Committee, and ultimately the general secretary: the current "leader for life," Xi Jinping.

Marxist socialism has replaced the Confucian-Legalist ideology that buttressed the traditional Chinese state. Xi Jinping and the Politburo, Central Committee, and Communist Party Congress represent the administrative arm of the modern state. The role played by Chinese traditions and religion, albeit marginal, is suggested by the current interpretation of "socialism with Chinese characteristics" that Xi Jinping is actively encouraging.

Among the six traditions/religions represented at the base of the hypothesized pyramid above, Legalism and Confucianism were most closely tied to authoritarianism in the imperial period and most easily reinforce the absolutist tendencies of Xi Jinping. Sinicized Buddhism (Han rather than Tibetan) and Sinicized Islam (that of the Hui rather than the Turkish-Uighur minority), by tradition, have been well integrated into Chinese culture and are not deemed as a threat unless Chinese socialism reverts to an intolerant mode. Given the checkered history of tolerance toward "foreign" religions in traditional China, tolerance is not assured but seems likely for the immediate future. Daoism, given

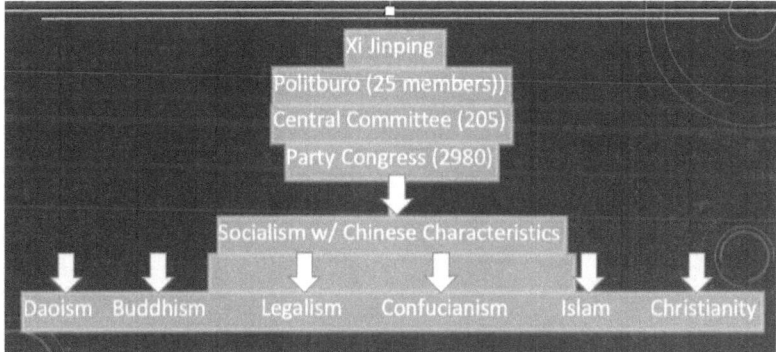

Figure 5.3. Contemporary authoritarian model of socialism with Chinese characteristics (inclusion of traditions/religions). Author provided.

its associations with "superstition"—a death knell in Chinese Marxist interpretations—and Christianity, given its association with the West, human rights agendas, and social activism, are both less favored by the Party. Still, Daoism and Christianity are currently valid forms of religious expression in China, so long as they abide by dictates stipulated by the Party. It is useful to recall the distinctions within religious traditions operable according to Party dictates, designating good, neutral, and bad religion within a single tradition.

To the extent that China's past (or some semblance of it) is indeed revived, Confucianism will likely bear the weight of the tradition's expectations. For centuries it served as a repository for what were viewed as core Chinese values, even when their origins might be traced elsewhere. The reinvention of Confucianism was successfully undertaken in the second millennium of the common era, and this reinvention process may serve as a guide for Confucianism's third iteration. If so, just as Neo-Confucians reconstructed a Confucian matrix built on challenges presented by Buddhist ideologies, New Confucianism may need to face squarely challenges presented by the complex of modernity. Failure to do so will result in a Confucian revival appealing only to those already "in the choir," regardless of how widely the membership might be extended. An authoritarian Confucianism that fails to acknowledge the advances made by various human rights agendas will fail, in my view, to capture the imagination and aspirations of the masses, and will only be viable as an instrument of control to the powerful. Is an open, liberal Confucianism possible? To ask this question invites another: is an open, liberal China possible? The answer may be yes, but only through a creative reimagining of Confucianism, the likes of which have not been seen for several centuries, when Song dynasty Neo-Confucians inspired a revived tradition that merged Confucian moral principles with an imaginative metaphysics stimulated by Buddhist and Daoist teachings. The question of a Chinese cultural revival based on Confucianism hinges on what kind of Confucianism will lead it.

Concluding Reflections

This is a crucial time for the future of the planet. The world faces ever-mounting ecological issues, crises of political confidence, widening income disparities, weakening of human rights agendas, the effect of new technologies and the emergence of the surveillance state, and increasing international conflicts and threats thereof. As the balance of economic and political power shifts toward Asia, can cultural influence be far behind? What does the economic, political, and cultural rise of China bode for the future?

The rise of China (and East Asia generally) forces us to ask many perplexing questions, challenging long-held assumptions. The primacy of the West, economically, politically, and culturally, has been normative since the rise of the current iteration of modernity itself. What does it mean when this primacy is no longer granted? What of the notion that market freedoms are inevitably tied to political freedoms, an article of faith among Western democracies, along with the belief that individual freedom is necessary to creativity and innovation? How will the battle between authoritarian rule and democracy determine the future of civilization? What of the environmental challenges we face and the role that China may play in contributing to or resolving them? In essence, who controls the future, and how will this control be determined? What effect will this have on our memory of the past?

The questions facing China are numerous and pertain not only to China but to the world as a whole. What will China's dispensation be in an emerging postliberal world order? Will it lead or support it, or will it work to demolish it and supplant it with something of its own making? Is the liberal order doomed to fade away, as China and others seem to presume, or will it experience a resurgence? Does China offer a viable alternative, one that other nations of the world will be persuaded to join? Will the persuasion be limited to economic incentives and political pressures, or can China offer a viable alternative that not only commands respect but also inspires? What of China's future? What role might the past play in it?

The first question to be raised regards the future of Marxism itself. With the fall of the Soviet Union, nations ruled by Marxist-based political systems were drastically reduced. China remains the only major country espousing Marxism as a ruling ideology and in spite of Xi Jinping's recent efforts to install Marxist curricula, it remains to be seen to what extent he will be effective in re-instilling Marxist principles to some semblance of their former influence. As I suggested in the previous chapter, it is more likely that the CCP will continue to turn to traditional teachings to buttress their authority. Under the rubric "socialism with Chinese characteristics," Marxist interpretations have evolved over time. Marx originally conceived his message for the industrialized capitalism of nineteenth-century Europe in terms of class struggle between the proletariat (industrial workers) and bourgeoisie (capitalist owners). As is well known, China did not replicate the model of industrialized Europe. The early Maoists reconceived class struggle to fit the terms of Chinese society, between peasant farmers and wealthy landowners. As a result, during the Mao period, Marxism was interpreted (or reinterpreted) as a proletarian peasant revolution that called for the state appropriation of the means of production, the formation of communes, and the destruction of family/clan authority. When Deng Xiaoping issued reforms in the 1980s, socialism with Chinese characteristics was recast to allow for economic expansion and tolerance toward the restrictions on religious expression. As China developed economically, the Marxist restrictions on capitalist investment and the acquisition of individual wealth were rescinded, China began to take on the features of a capitalist, even hyper-capitalist society, even though state control of economic development remained. By the 2000s, when liberalizing tendencies under the leadership of Jiang Zemin and Hu Jintao emerged, many in the West hoped that the prediction of economic liberalization leading to political openness would be realized. When Xi Jinping assumed power, socialism with Chinese characteristics took an unexpected turn with assertions of compatibility between Party principles and traditional Chinese (especially Confucian) values. This represented a reversal of decades of vilification of Confucius as the archenemy of China, the perpetrator of a privileged class and purveyor of a value system that endorsed feudal regimes and outmoded customs that prevented China's modernization. Other religions and traditions, were seen, likewise, as contributing to an old culture inhibiting China's progress.

Given the evolution of Marxism in China, its future there is tied to three related factors. On the one hand, Marxism continues as a pretext for Chinese nationalism, and the Party frequently invokes nationalist sentiments to support its cause. There appears to be little Chinese appetite for differentiating between the Marxist state and the Chinese nation. In addition, Marxism serves the Party's admiration for authoritarianism, whether it be Mao's "power comes from the barrel of a gun" remark or Deng's order to send in military troops to quash student rebellion in Tiananmen. Finally, there is the possibility that Marxism will continue to evolve into the resumption of a Confucian-Legalist state. Certainly, as noted in the last chapter, the Confucian-Legalist legacy is already being called on to buttress support for the Party.

While authoritarian rule in China seems certain, at least for the foreseeable future, what are the prospects for democratic institutions? While some observers, like former Singaporean president Lee Kwan Yu, assert that democracy can never take hold in China, that the adoption of democratic principles would mean the death of China itself, we have seen Chinese populations like Taiwan and Hong Kong (until very recently) successfully embrace democracy. We have seen "Confucian"-based cultures like Japan and South Korea successfully embrace democracy. Democratic institutions, as a result, have been successfully planted in East Asia. In all these cases, however, the countries have been tutored under US and Western institutional frameworks, absorbed into the post–World War II liberal democratic political and economic order.

The real question may pivot around the future of liberal democracy itself. The challenges posed by authoritarian rule represent the critical civilizational challenge of today's world. Is authoritarian rule destined for the twenty-first century? While Vladimir Putin of Russia and Xi Jinping of China present a tandem of world leaders in major countries that openly embrace authoritarian rule, there are numerous others, from North Korea to Brazil, Hungary, Turkey, the Philippines, and India, that are following suit in various degrees. The Economist Intelligence Unit's Democracy Index in January 2018 showed declining scores for more than half the countries in 2017.[1] Freedom House titled its 2018 annual report on freedom around the world "Democracy in Crisis," concluding that freedom had declined for the twelfth consecutive year, with seventy-one countries suffering "net declines in civil and political liberties."[2] The question joined by Viola Gienger, assessing these trends in an issue *Just Security*, is "will the global march of authoritarianism turn into a stampede?"[3] Even the United States, under the leadership of former president Donald Trump, expressed open infatuation with authoritarian dictators. As the leader of the post–World War II world political order, the United States under Trump rendered this order somewhat leaderless, raising the question: whither democracy without a world leader? Any semblance of a world order based on a coalition of nations framed by liberal-democratic principles has deteriorated increasingly into US unilateral actions backed by its military superiority, with either reluctant or no support from even its staunchest allies. It remains to be seen how much the Biden administration can quell this tide and to what extent Biden's attempt to revive old coalitions will be extended into the future, especially given the current disarray in the Republican Party, beholden as it has become to the rhetoric of white supremacy.

The trend toward authoritarianism does not bode well for the future of international relations. When rulers rely on authoritarian policies to ensure domestic compliance, they inadvertently inspire rigid attitudes that do not translate well into the international sphere. Authoritarian regimes often breed nationalisms and ethnic identities that are averse to the compromises necessary to reducing tendencies toward conflict between nations. To the extent that nations treat each other as alien competitors, they plant the seeds of potential conflict. An authoritarian China may not aspire to conflict but claims on the South China Sea and Taiwan in the name of Chinese national sovereignty may make this difficult to avoid.

And what of China's remarkable economic ascendancy? Can it continue? Can it serve as inspiration for the model of the future, even beyond China? China suffered over a century of economic suppression from the mid-nineteenth to the late twentieth centuries. Confronting the forces of imperialism and the drive of other countries (England, the United States, France, Germany, and Japan) to colonize China for their own economic benefit, China was left with little choice but to capitulate. China was able to reformulate itself after the fall of the last imperial dynasty, the Qing, and the assumption of parliamentary democracy in the Republican period in 1912, but it soon deteriorated into warlordism and civil war. Relief came in the form of Communist victory in 1949, but Mao's version of socialism resulted in economic stagnation and further deterioration. When Deng instituted economic reforms in the 1980s there was much to be done. A whole society was rebuilt upon the rubble and decay of a past that had seen little in the way of development. Seen from this perspective, the impressive development in China over the last forty years was somewhat inevitable. The resurgence of China's economy has precipitated the resumption of its natural place in the economic world order. Now that China has been rebuilt, the question is: to what extent can it sustain its "economic miracle"? It will be difficult to continue industrial expansion in China based on domestic demand.

The BRI is a global development strategy adopted by the Chinese government in 2013 involving infrastructure development and investments in nearly seventy countries and international organizations in Asia, Europe, and Africa, designed to usher in a new China-led era of trade and economic growth. It can be viewed in part as a strategy to bolster and maintain the same domestic industries that are instrumental to its completion.[4] In this way, the BRI may be seen as a mechanism to extend the over-surplus of domestic capacity into the international arena, for both economic and political goals. It is one of the most ambitious infrastructure projects ever conceived, designed to significantly expand China's economic and political influence. BRI is the centerpiece of China's quest for a China-centric twenty-first century. As Bethany Allen-Ebrahimian notes, "With the U.S. paralyzed by political gridlock and western institutions stagnating, China is positioning itself as the primary architect of new power structures in the twenty-first century,"[5] and this as a direct consequence of Xi Jinping's BRI initiative to put China at the center of global economic and geopolitical relationships. As countries reliant on BRI for economic growth turn to Beijing for infrastructure, trade, science, and military project investments, Chinese administrative alternatives to Western-led institutions and global norms are emerging and drawing country after country into the new global framework. As Allen-Ebrahimian further contends, "The BRI is strengthened by Beijing's efforts to co-opt the World Bank and other institutions and to interfere in the politics of democratic countries. . . . Its ultimate goal is the 'creation of an alternative world order.'"[6]

For the past seventy years, corporate behavior has been shaped by Western-style capitalism, Western laws and regulations, and the volatilities of Western markets. As Allen-Ebrahimian asserts, "China is the first non-Western, authoritarian country with both the market size and the will to reshape the behavior of multinational companies, and even Western governments, to better fit its own interests."⁷ If faced with a choice between profits and ideology, multinational companies will surely choose the former.

But what happens when the economic party is over, when the factors precipitating China's unprecedented economic expansion dissolve and the laws of a volatile market economy inevitably take over? China hopes that BRI will forestall economic decline. If successful (which is doubtful, as many BRI projects have been met with funding issues and the default of loans to partner countries), economic decline may be avoided, at least for a while. Chinese economic history only serves to confirm the vagaries of the market: that economic prosperity and decline are the inescapable order of the day. One can argue that we have been here before, with Japan's spectacular rise following the debacle of defeat in World War II. On the literal rubble of this defeat, Japan rebuilt the infrastructure of its society over the course of a few decades, not unlike China's recent experience. Following the heady days of the 1980s when many predicted that Japan, based on its economic might, would lead the future, some projected a new Japan-centric (*Pax Japonica*) global economic and geopolitical order. But the country fell into a prolonged period of economic stagnation from which it has yet to recover. Many factors separate China's experience from Japan's in spite of these overall similarities, not the least of which is the sheer size of China compared to Japan; however, Japan's example reminds us that the road to economic prosperity is not one of assured ascendance. Recessions are the order of the day in normal economic cycles and while they may be periodically circumvented in cases like Japan following World War II and China following decades of conflict and stagnation, they will inevitably return. How will the Chinese populace respond to a government that no longer assures economic growth and prosperity?

It is a truism that any government delivering strong economic indicators, producing tangible advances in the quality of people's lives, will enjoy massive support from the populace. The reverse is also true—when governments fail to deliver economically, especially when people have come to expect prosperity, they will incur the displeasure and wrath of their people. In democracies, economic performance is a strong indicator of success or failure in an election. Without an electoral process that presents viable alternatives, China resorts to past mechanisms to manage political change—the dynastic cycle of social unrest, repression, and ultimately armed revolution. Currently, it is hard to imagine a scenario in China such as this. But there will come a point when the situation in China where there is no mechanism in place to manage its deterioration. Up to this point, change has been managed from within the Party; it is the Party's ability to maneuver from within that has continued to make it viable. The Party's evolution within the parameters of socialism with Chinese characteristics exhibits its ability to remain viable within changing social dynamics.

One of the questions dogging China's ability to continue its economic expansion and contribute to international leadership revolves around its capacity for innovation. The prevailing Western belief is that without individual freedom, innovation is impossible. During its cycle of industrial development, China has been accused of being a nation of imitators, or worse, thieves of Western technology, and that China's expansion rests on the achievements of others, without which China is incapable of advancing. The same accusation was made of Japan during its rise after World War II. It is natural for societies in a rebuilding stage to rely on existing technology. It is also reasonable to ask whether, once rebuilt, these societies can innovate on their own. Anyone with passing familiarity with East Asia, and especially China, will know that China and Chinese-influenced civilizations have a long and enviable history of invention, scientific discovery, and innovation.[8] The issue of the role of innovation in Chinese societies that encouraged the preservation of tradition was enjoined early on. Confucius, who innovated in the name of preserving tradition, famously stated, "I transmit but do not innovate,"[9] and this became associated with a Chinese preference toward stasis. On the other hand, the Confucian classic, the *Book of Rites* proclaims: "There are those who are able to innovate, those who are able to transmit. The innovators are regarded as sages; the transmitters as intelligent."[10] On these directives, China surely valued innovation, whether directly or indirectly. Still, it could be, as some have suggested, that Chinese innovations are linked especially to periods of disunion, when there was more free thinking and less government control over people's lives.[11] Although it is true that the Western creativity and innovations that led to the Renaissance, scientific discovery, and the industrial revolution were built around the freedom of the individual, it is not true that the Western iteration is universal. While individual freedom may be a factor in the ability to create and innovate, the processes of creativity are infinitely complex and are not reducible to any one factor. This is a topic that obviously deserves much more attention, and China's rise may help precipitate the kind of cultural dialogue that could help clarify social and cultural factors that either inhibit or enhance the capacity for innovation.

Can China inspire? The concept of the "Chinese Dream" promoted by the CCP is very similar to the idea of the "American Dream." It emphasizes an entrepreneurial spirit and exalts the generation of self-made men and women in postreform China who moved to the urban centers as rural immigrants and achieved great improvement in their standard of living and social well-being. Unlike the American Dream, which is couched in the glory of individual accomplishment, the Chinese Dream represents the collective consciousness of the Chinese people during an era of recent social transformation and economic progress. It is a notion conceived and promoted by the Party. It is not about individual ideational aspirations but about collective relationships, as in the slogan "myriad blessings to myriad families, collectively fulfill the Chinese Dream." As a Party initiative, the Chinese Dream was linked to two goals: the material goal of China becoming a "moderately well-off society" by 2021, the hundredth anniversary of the CCP, and the modernization goal of China becoming fully developed by about 2049, the hundredth anniversary of the founding of the People's Republic. These goals help provide a timeline to CCP thinking about present and future aspirations. In spite of Party rhetoric to the contrary, the emergence of the notion of the Chinese Dream indicates a diversion of political ideology from egalitarianism to a relatively more libertarian individualist approach. As an aspect of political thought in contemporary China, it is worth noting the tension the concept evokes between a collective dream of the people of China and the individual aspirations for economic and social progress. How this tension is exhibited and managed may very well be a significant indicator of the future direction of Chinese society. The future of China's Communist Party leadership is tied to being able to continue to offer Chinese Dream aspirations to increasing numbers of people entering the middle class. Recent pronouncements by Xi Jinping aimed at curbing the excesses and corrupt tendencies of the entrepreneurial and entertainment classes underscore this tendency toward collective well-being over individual accomplishment.

Allow me to end with the following thoughts. It is time for deep reflection; we are at a moment of pivotal civilizational change, the likes of which the modern world has not seen. In significant ways, the future will not be like the immediate past. As noted above, observers like Lee Kwan Yu insisted that China can never be a democracy, that to become so would mean the end of China. Yet, we have seen Chinese populations like Taiwan successfully embrace democracy. We have seen "Confucian"-influenced cultures like Japan and South Korea successfully embrace democracy. In all these cases, however, the countries have been tutored under US and Western institutional frameworks, absorbed into the post–World War II liberal democratic political and economic order. China is determined not to follow this model but to go its own way, whether by socialism with Chinese characteristics or the Chinese Dream. These would be idle pronouncements except for the means to put them into action. The fortunes of history, those forces that we can only heed but exert little control over, suggest that the return of China and Asia is not a passing fancy but a crucial resumption of a world order that is both old and new. The past couple of centuries, when Asian countries have been dormant, have been an aberration that we have mistaken as normative. We must learn to abide by the new model and work to influence it in as positive a direction as is humanly possible. The future of China's past, like the rise of China itself, represents not so much a problem as an opportunity. To enjoy the ride, we must first understand it. To understand it, we must be prepared to evolve. To evolve, we must learn, and learning is, in the first place, engagement. I hope that this book in some small way has helped to facilitate this process.

Epilogue

Contemporary events in China (as of February 2020) have brought some salient aspects of the analyses put forward in the current volume into focus. COVID-19, which spread from its epicenter in Wuhan and brought much of China to a halt, has provoked a strong outcry from the Chinese populace and a public criticism of the government that is seldom seen. Chief among these is an extensive essay penned by Tsinghua University professor of law Xu Zhangrun, "Viral Alarm: When Fury Overcomes Fear."[1] Xu is a well-known Chinese liberal with a PhD from the University of Melbourne and a staunch critic of Xi Jinping. In July 2018, Xu published an essay, "Imminent Fears, Immediate Hopes," criticizing recent policy shifts like the Communist Party instituting general secretary Xi Jinping as "leader for life" (like Mao Zedong) and restoring a cult of personality.[2] In April 2019, Xu was prevented from leaving the country. After his most recent critique, Xu has been silenced by the government: his social media posts have been removed from viewing, his WeChat account has been suspended, his name has been removed from Weibo, and he is presumed to be under house arrest.[3]

Xu's style belies the future of China's past. In traditional China, members of the *Ru* class, particularly those from prominent literati families or in senior government positions, had the privilege and obligation of contesting government decisions and policies by issuing "memorials to the throne." Often referred to as "remonstrances," the memorials took the tone of bitter laments regarding the state of society and its moral decay under current rule, with an augur of a dynasty's imminent downfall. In issuing his jeremiads, Xu invokes the style of a latter-day *Ru* in this hallowed tradition of Chinese literati. Xu's brazen attacks on the Chinese government threw into stark relief the tensions between the liberal order and Xi Jinping's China:

> Ours is a system in which The Ultimate Arbiter [an imperial-era term used by state media to describe Xi Jinping] monopolizes power. It results in what I call "organizational discombobulation" that, in turn, has served to enable a dangerous "systemic impotence" at every level. A political culture has thereby been nurtured that, in terms of the real public good, is ethically bankrupt, for it is one that strains to vouchsafe its privatized Party-State . . . while abandoning the people over which it holds sway to suffer the vicissitudes of a cruel fate. It is a system that turns every natural disaster into an even greater man-made catastrophe. The coronavirus epidemic has revealed the rotten core of Chinese governance; the fragile and vacuous heart of the jittering edifice of state has thereby shown up as never before.[4]

Xu concludes with a warning: "The level of popular fury is volcanic and a people thus enraged may, in the end, also cast aside their fear." While the COVID pandemic, at this juncture (late 2021), is unlikely to evoke the torrent of rage that Xu envisioned, it invokes the specter of China's traditional dynastic cycle as the mechanism of political change based on dissatisfaction, leading to revolt, from the Chinese masses. By assuming the authority of an emperor ("leader for life") and the totalitarian policies of Legalist statecraft that stifle and punish all critique, Xi Jinping inspires the very revolution he seeks to avoid. Regardless of the outcome of the current dissatisfaction among the Chinese people with their government, Xu's missive reminds us that, lacking other means to express their political will, it is only a matter of time until the masses rise up to reassert their traditional role in overthrowing the government. What might provoke such an event? There is no way to predict the precise sequence of events that might lead to the overthrow of any state, except in general terms. While the dissatisfaction of the masses is not in itself unusual, for it to boil over into armed insurrection is rare. Economic prosperity mitigates such an occurrence. As I suggested earlier, the most important factor predicting massive dissatisfaction is economic—when poverty reaches a level that results in an undermining of the social fabric, the situation may become critical. We must remember, however, that the CCP has withstood conditions of extreme poverty in the populace—famine and loss of life—earlier in its history, to a degree that might seem untenable elsewhere. One thing seems clear: the cause of transformation in China, if such an event were to occur, is unlikely to be driven by ideology. Many in the West are inclined to adhere to ideas of transformation in China inspired by notions of freedom, independence, and human rights. These ideas may appeal to a rather narrow spectrum of Chinese intellectuals but are unlikely to be enough to foster real transformation on their own (as they were not in the so-called democracy movement in Tiananmen Square in 1989). They may accompany and bolster other reform movements. For example, the New Culture movement of the 1920s, foundational for China's transformation to current iterations of modernity, was rooted in intellectual discourses of the period, providing rationales for wide social dissatisfaction and unrest.

The specter of political change in China is also inhibited by the increasing effectiveness of public security and surveillance. The policing of the hearts and minds of the Chinese populace grows unabated through restrictions on extracurricular tutoring of students, limitations on time children spend on video games, condemnations on displays of wealth and celebrity culture, on approved expressions of gender (e.g., only manly males need apply), and so on, a list that only seems to grow by the day. Internet surveillance operates as a kind of thought police that monitors otherwise private chat group discussions. Modern technologies only serve to increase the reach of an absolutist state, bolstered by a Legalist-inspired agenda, to define its national interest in ever narrow terms and to regulate its people according to the specific norms it advocates.

Another possibility is that the CCP continues to evolve as a one-party state ruled by different factions that vie for power internally and exercise somewhat alternate versions of statehood and statecraft. This has been the story of the CCP thus far. Mao Zedong's authoritarian regime that dictated state policy and micromanaged it down to the village level ultimately ended in the disaster of the Cultural Revolution. This event gave way to the more moderate governance of Deng Xiaoping, which allowed for economic expansion, and continued in the policies of Jiang Zemin and Hu Jintao. Xi Jinping's return to more centralized and absolutist rule represents the victory of Party factions more closely aligned in many ways to Mao. Where Xi's regime differs radically from his predecessor is in his invocation of China's past traditions in the service of the CCP and the modern Chinese state. The impact and prospects of this radical turn for China and the world's future has been the subject of this book. Might future iterations of the CCP draw differently on the resources that these traditions offer and if so, to what effect? A recent advocate of return to Deng's more moderate model came from a standard bearer of Chinese nationalism, Wang Xiaodong, who has renounced China's attitude of triumphalism and policy of decoupling from the United States and its allies, maintaining that the price for China is too high.[5] When thinking of China's future and its impact upon the world, there are two main questions that remain central to the discussion: Which iteration of China will emerge? And which aspects of China's past will inform its future?

Postscript
A Brief Note on Race and Ethnicity

Since I initially drafted this manuscript, when it was in the initial review stage, discussion about race and ethnicity, and the role of colonialism have risen with hitherto unforeseen fervor. These have erupted in the United States and other Western countries, given their legacies of racism rooted in a colonial past that is part and parcel of the Westernization of the globe and thus the current iteration of modernity itself. Given this context, it would appear to have little to do with China, but given the current influence that China is exerting around the world and the prospect of continued if not greater influence in the future, China's past attitudes toward different races and ethnicities is a timely topic with present and future consequences. While I am no expert in this area, allow me to make some observations, if for no other reason than to bring the topic to the table and provoke further discussion.

I begin with the notion of ethnicity. Following Jonathan Hall, who writes on ethnic identity in Greek antiquity, even though ethnicity may have a strong biological component, it is fundamentally a constructed category grounded in shared myths of descent and a shared association with a specific territory. As such, it is an open and malleable social construction determined by time and place.[1] This belies the conception of China as an ethno-nationalist state dominated by one race, the Han.

Chinese classical works central to the Confucian tradition perceive the world as *tianxia* (all under Heaven), oriented toward a homogenous community termed the "great harmony" (*datong*). The creation of this community entailed the negation of meaningful racial and ethnic differences, which were transformed under benevolent Chinese influences dictated by an elite representing the superiority of Han values, "using Chinese ways to transform the barbarians," under the assumption that the barbarian could be transformed into Han (*hanhua*).[2] The same classical Chinese works envision the Han as surrounded by different racial groups in dire need of transformation. These eventually were codified into four groups: Yi in the east, Man in the south, Rong in the west, and Di in the north. These, in turn, were each associated with a color: east (green), south (red), west (white), and north (black), with the center reserved for yellow. Regardless of this crude reductionism, ancient Chinese definitely exhibited color with race, describing the red or black Di, the white or black Man, and the pitch-dark Lang. The associations were not neutral but were accompanied by descriptions of barbaric customs regarding appearance and clothing attire, culinary preferences, and social behaviors,[3] all of which were intended to distinguish them from the Han as bearers of true civilization based on moral principles and refined etiquette. Following a canonical work of classical Confucianism,[4] the world was divided into five concentric areas, centered in the imperial palaces, encompassed by the royal domains and princely fiefdoms. These mark the Han territory of civilization proper, beyond which is the zone of pacification, where peoples and territories are in the process of *hanhua*: being transformed into Han. Beyond these are wasteland regions marked by drought, famine, and savagery (see figure P.1).

The greatest challenge to this presumed Han Chinese superiority came in the form of Buddhism, brought to China by immigrants and pilgrims from greater India and Central Asia. Buddhism made few inroads into China outside urban émigré communities until after the fall of the Han dynasty (220 CE), which resulted in the precipitous decline of Confucianism, the ideology Han rulers had allegedly based their ascendancy on. Subsequent invasions by northern non-Han Xiongnu (proto-Hun?) "barbarians" furthered the spatial and cultural dislocation felt by the Han elite, who were forced to retreat south into the frontier and to contemplate a new existence deprived of their belief in an inviolable original homeland. This led to existential questions among the defeated Han. How could they suffer defeat from peoples who were inherently inferior, deprived as they were of the true principles of enlightened civilization? Of what use was Confucianism without an empire to rule over? This questioning of Confucian superiority invited dialogue with other ways of thinking focused less on political and social order and more on individual spiritual fulfillment. In this environment, the Han elite

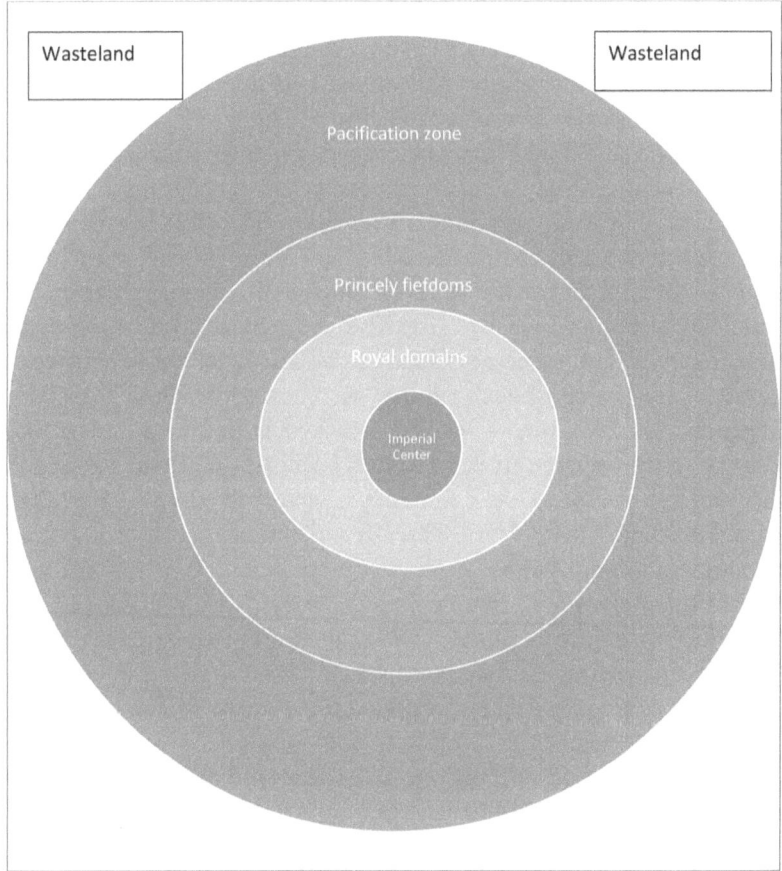

Figure P.1. Territorial demarcations associated with Han civilization. Author provided.

began to entertain questions about the nature and purpose of human existence—of what use were discussions about the "good society" when the ordained structure of society itself seemed to hang in the balance? As a result, the Han elite turned increasingly to Daoism and Buddhism in search of meaningful answers to their questions. This turn led to one of the greatest cultural clashes in human history, whereby the alien Buddhist tradition became assimilated and indigenized, leading to both the Indianization of China and the Sinification of Buddhism.[5]

The interactions between Indian-based Buddhist ideas and Chinese-based Confucian culture continued over the centuries and produced a variety of responses too numerous to account for here. In short, these may be reduced to pro-Confucian or pro-Buddhist. The pro-Buddhist camps alleged the superiority of Buddhist teaching, typically suggesting a subsidiary role for Confucian teaching. The pro-Confucian camps tended toward anti-Buddhism, sometimes virulently so, suggesting that an alien teaching from a barbarian people had nothing useful to offer Chinese. Its existence on Chinese soil was a blight on the homeland, to be exterminated as soon as possible, a position in keeping with the notion that Chinese may transform barbarians into moral beings through Confucian teachings (*hanhua*). To think that the opposite was possible was untenable. The successful Buddhist response, for those who would allow it, was what of a Buddhism that accommodated Han values, or an indigenized form of Chinese Buddhism (a *hanhua* Buddhism, if you will)? In terms of the above, this is a form of Buddhism that had entered the "pacification zone," so to speak, and became absorbed into the Han cultural realm. To be sure, many Han refused to tolerate any form of Buddhism, strictly maintaining that as a result of its foreign origins it was forever resigned to its alien fate. But for many Chinese, such transformed types of Buddhism came to represent legitimate expressions of native values. One could reconstruct the Chinese struggle with Western modernity as a resumption of such debates between the alienness versus legitimacy of a foreign ideology.

After the period of Buddhist ascendance, from the Song dynasty onward Chinese attitudes toward race and ethnicity were shaped by confrontations with rival groups from the north, who threatened and at times succeeded in taking control of the Middle Kingdom. During the Song dynasty, the Jurchen established the Jin dynasty (1115–1234) and succeeded in invading the north, forcing the Han to retreat to the south of the Yangzi, to continue as the Southern Song dynasty (1127–1279). The Mongols, under the leadership of Kublai Khan, took control over the entire territory of China to establish the Yuan dynasty (1271–1368). Following this, the Ming dynasty (1368–1644) reestablished Han control, only to be ousted by the Manchus, who established the Qing dynasty (1644–1912). As disruptive to Han superiority this parade of intruders might seem, the fact is that all the dynasties, Han or not, were guided by Confucian governance (albeit in a Neo-Confucian iteration). Rather than a challenge to Han supremacy, the underlying ideology crafted by elite Han prevailed under the claim of a cultural universalism whereby the barbarian could be "Sinicized" and transformed by the beneficial influences of a superior culture.[6] This sense of cultural superiority mitigated the inherent differences and presumed inferiority characteristic of the invading peoples.

However transformed through the lenses of modern racial theory, these traditional Chinese attitudes remain prevalent in dealing with outsiders and particularly its own ethnic minorities.[7] They are especially evident, for example, in contemporary policies toward Uyghurs and Tibetans, where claims of cultural identity based on distinct religious values are dismissed, often with a brutality reminiscent of a Legalist-inspired state. A Human Rights Foundation report presents as its first main takeaway the following: "The CCP aspires to create a society perfectly molded to the ideological tenets of Xi Jinping or what the CCP refers to as the 'Chinese Dream' and 'national rejuvenation'—a society that is *sinocentric, socialist, and homogenous*. Religious and cultural plurality are seen as hindrances to the CCP's policy of assimilation" (emphasis in original).[8] To be fair, current Chinese justifications about bringing civilization to Tibet and Xinjiang has a ring of the "white man's burden" rhetoric used by colonial powers in the nineteenth and twentieth centuries to justify policies of assimilation and the cultural annihilation of native peoples. When belief in the superiority of one's culture becomes entrenched, history proves it hard to avoid such justifications and the actions that come with them, however deplorable. The unfortunate history of Western colonialism provides ample cover for current Chinese policies toward their own minorities and non-Han ethnic groups. We can only hope that more "enlightened" (I use this term somewhat ironically, as it was the Western Enlightenment that provided the rationale for cultural superiority that precipitated the abhorrent policies in the first place) Chinese thinkers rise to the fore and reconsider the rationale for their actions. So long as the Legalist authoritarian state remains in force and ideological thinking prompted by cultural differences is not tolerated, we can only anticipate further aggressive measures to enforce compliance.

I don't want to leave on an overly negative note. Regardless of current circumstances, governments change as do the policies they espouse. The current trend toward authoritarian regimes around the world will also pass, as will China's. While authoritarian regimes in particular present an iron-clad front, the possibility for other perspectives exist. What follows from one ruler to the next remains to be seen. The possibilities, as I have tried to show in this volume, are manifold, and China's current posture under Xi's regime is not the only or presumably the best hope for China and the world's future.

Notes

Introduction

1. "Li Zehou, The Confucian World." https://web.archive.org/web/20100530093301/http://www.coloradocollege.edu/Academics/Anniversary/Participants/Li.htm

2. Li Zehou, "The Western Is the Substance, and the Chinese Is for Application": (Excerpts), *Contemporary Chinese Thought*, 31, no. 2 (1999): 32–39, DOI: 10.2753/CSP1097-1467310232.

3. *Japan as Number One: Lessons for America* (Cambridge, MA: Harvard University Press, 1979).

4. The Belt and Road Initiative (BRI) is a global infrastructure development strategy adopted by the Chinese government in 2013 to invest in nearly seventy countries and international organizations. It is a central component of Xi Jinping's diplomacy strategy, which calls for China to assume a greater leadership role for global affairs in accordance with its rising power and status. See https://eng.yidaiyilu.gov.cn.

5. The Asian Infrastructure Investment Bank (AIIB) was proposed by China in 2013 and launched in Beijing in 2014. It is a multilateral development bank with over one hundred members, that aims to improve economic and social conditions in Asia. See https://www.aiib.org.

6. The Shanghai Cooperation Organization (SCO) is a political, economic, and security alliance covering Eurasian regions, the world's largest in terms of geographic scope. It extends over three-fifths of the Eurasian continent, includes 40 percent of the world's population and more than 20 percent of global GDP. See http://eng.sectsco.org.

Chapter One

1. For an overview with bibliography, see Jason Clower's entry "Mou Zongsan" in *Internet Encyclopedia of Philosophy*, https://www.iep.utm.edu/zongsan/ (accessed December 29, 2018).

2. *Life Magazine*, no. 14, December 1988, http://www.maryellenmark.com/text/magazines/life/905W-000-037.html. See also Robert Neville, *Boston Confucianism* (Albany: State University of New York Press, 2000); and John Berthrong, "A Sermon: Exploring the Dao," https://open.bu.edu/bitstream/handle/2144/49/20001022-exploring_the_dao_.htm?sequence=1&isAllowed=y (accessed October 22, 2000).

3. In the interest of transparency, I, along with Carol Quin, professor of philosophy (Metropolitan State University of Denver), Bryan Van Norden (Vassar College), and Stephen C. Angle (Wesleyan University), delivered featured talks or keynotes at the conference. The title of my paper was "Lessons from the Past: A Prospectus on Ruist Models and Agendas for the 21st Century."

4. HarperCollins, reissued by Waveland Press, 1988.

5. Fingarette, *Confucius: The Secular as Sacred*, vii–viii.

6. On the Jesuit missions in China, see two works by David E. *Mungello*: Curious Land: Jesuit Accommodation and the Origins of Sinology (Honolulu: University of Hawaii Press (1989) and *The Great Encounter of China and the West, 1500–1800* (Lanham, MD: Rowman & Littlefield, 2005). Also see John Parker, *Windows into China: The Jesuits and Their Books, 1580–1730* (Boston: Trustees of the Public Library of the City of Boston, 1978). There is general agreement that Jesuit scholarship on China had considerable influence on European thinkers of the period, particularly Enlightenment thinkers like Voltaire, who sought an alternate basis for society than Christianity.

7. As I concluded in my conference paper, "Lessons from the Past: A Prospectus on Ruist Models and Agendas for the 21st Century": "The point is not to brand Neo-Confucianism as imitative and unoriginal, but to the contrary, to suggest that its success was predicated on the creative responses it made to the challenges presented by the new Buddhist agendas. Neo-Confucian success may ultimately be attributed to an ability to adapt core Confucian orientations and moral principles to unforeseen, unimagined agendas."

8. *The Rise of Modern China*, Oxford University Press (1st edition, 1970; 6th edition, 2000).

9. See Karl Marx and Frederick Engels, *The German Ideology Part One, with Selections from Parts Two and Three, together with Marx's "Introduction to a Critique of Political Economy"* (New York: International, 2001).

10. English translation with preface and postscript, by Perry Link, http://www.chinafile.com/library/nyrb-china-archive/chinas-charter-08.

11. More recently the government of Xi Jinping, in an attempt to enforce more rigid control over perceived ideological excesses, cracked down hard on those who advocated Western notions of constitutional democracy. Starting on July 9, 2015, human rights lawyers and activists were jailed in the notorious "709" crackdown, when around three hundred were rounded up or harassed.

12. Nicholas Kristof, "Legacy of Mao called 'Great Disaster,'" https://www.nytimes.com/1989/02/07/world/legacy-of-mao-called-great-disaster.html.

13. "Controversial Confucius Statue Vanishes from Tiananmen," https://www.reuters.com/article/us-china-conficius/controversial-confucius-statue-vanishes-from-tiananmen-idUSTRE73L0Y420110422.

14. Refer to Chiang Kai-shek image at Tiananmen.

15. Paraphrase of a conversation with an anonymous official at the Conference on the Biographical Literature concerning Confucius and Mencius; Qufu, China (December 7, 2011).

16. Andrew Jacobs, "Confucius Statue Vanishes Near Tiananmen," April 22, 2011, https://www.nytimes.com/2011/04/23/world/asia/23confucius.html.

17. A case in point is Mongolia, situated between Russia and China, whose capital, Ulaanbaatar, centers on Chinggis Khaan (Genghis Khan) Square, named for the notorious founder of the thirteenth- and fourteenth-century Mongol Empire. The Mongolian People's Republic lasted until shortly after the collapse of the Soviet Union in 1989, and up to this time the square was dedicated to socialist monuments.

18. "Confucianism and the Chinese Communist Party: Facts and Details," http://factsanddetails.com/china/cat3/sub9/entry-4319.html.

19. In the interests of transparency, I am a member of the International Confucian Association and was in attendance during Xi Jinping's unanticipated keynote address.

20. http://www.lcrosschina.com/news/2014/0925/3834.shtml.

21. It also bears noting that Xi's predecessor, Hu Jintao, also stressed the need to enhance Chinese culture as the country's "soft power" in his keynote speech to the Seventeenth National Congress of the CCP in 2007. See http://en.people.cn/90002/92169/92187/6283148.html.

22. "China Commemorates Confucius with Ceremony," *China.org* (website), Xinhua, September 25, 2014, http://www.china.org.cn/china/2014-09/25/content_33608222.htm.

23. Nathan Gardels, "Xi Launches Cultural Counter-Revolution to Restore Confucianism as China's Ideology," Huffington Post, September 29, 2014, https://www.huffingtonpost.com/nathan-gardels/xi-jinping-confucianism_b_5897680.html.

24. Daniel Bell is the author of numerous books including *The China Model: Political Meritocracy and the Limits of Democracy* (2015), *China's New Confucianism: Politics and Everyday Life in a Changing Society* (2010), *Beyond Liberal Democracy: Political Thinking for an East Asian Context* (2006), and *East Meets West: Human Rights and Democracy in East Asia* (2000), all published by Princeton University Press. Bell is also the author of *Communitarianism and Its Critics* (1993). He is the series editor of a translation series by Princeton University Press that aims to translate the most influential and original works of Chinese scholars (http://

press.princeton.edu/catalogs/series/title/the-princeton-china-series.html). He is also the editor of *Confucian Political Ethics* and the coeditor of four books with Cambridge University Press, including (with Chenyang Li) *The East Asian Challenge for Democracy: Political Meritocracy in a Comparative Context* (2013). Bell also writes widely on Chinese politics and philosophy for the media.

25. See "The Dao of Pandemic," *The Useless Tree* (website), January 2011, https://uselesstree.typepad.com/useless_tree/2011/01/confucius-in-beijing.html.

26. "Xi Jinping: How to Read Confucius and Other Chinese Classical Thinkers," *China Daily.com* (website), http://www.chinadaily.com.cn/china/xismoments/2017-05/12/content_29324341.htm.

27. See Confucius Institute, http://www.kongziyjy.org/plus/list.php?tid=51.

28. "China Names Top 100 Fugitives Suspected of Corruption," Associated Press, https://www.voanews.com/a/ap-china-names-its-top-100-fugitives-suspected-of-corruption/2731460.html. Photos of the hundred fugitives were published in *China Daily*, http://www.chinadaily.com.cn/china/2015-04/23/content_20521796.htm.

29. Kuo, Lily, "Student Says Peking University Trying to Silence Her Over Rape Petition," *Guardian*, April 24, 2018.

30. "The Guangdong Model," *Economist*, November 26, 2011, https://www.economist.com/asia/2011/11/26/the-guangdong-model.

31. *Esther Wang*, "Young Chinese #MeToo and Labor Rights Activist Has Been Missing for Weeks after Being Detained by Police." *Jezebel*, https://jezebel.com/young-chinese-metoo-and-labor-rights-activist-has-been-1829716238; "50 Student Activists Missing in China after Police Raid," *Guardian*, August 24, 2018, https://www.theguardian.com/world/2018/aug/24/50-student-activists-missing-in-china-after-police-raid.

32. "China's Disappeared: Some of the People Who Vanished at the Hands of the Chinese State in 2018," CBC News, Associated Press, December 30, 2018, https://www.cbc.ca/news/world/china-disappeared-2018-1.4962007.

33. Outlined at http://www.xinhuanet.com/english/2018-03/17/c_137046261.htm.

34. See "Jinping Sends Congratulatory Message," Xinhuanet (website), http://www.xinhuanet.com/english/2018-05/04/c_137156127.htm.

35. Translated by *China Digital Times*, https://chinadigitaltimes.net/2018/08/no-one-can-resist-the-tides-of-history-detained-activist-yue-xin-on-the-jasic-workers/.

36. *South China Morning Post*, May 24, 2018; updated May 25, https://www.scmp.com/news/china/policies-politics/article/2147487/why-beijing-isnt-marxist-enough-chinas-radical.

37. An intriguing rebuttal in Xue Yin's letter to President Xi references the role of the May Fourth movement:

They [CCP leaders] say: The May 4th Movement was anti-government. When you clamor about the spirit of the May 4th Movement, are you seeking to create an anti-government student movement? They also say: The workers' "Internationale" is a reactionary song. When students should study Marxism and Mao Zedong Thought, are there foreign forces supporting this in the background, hiding their true motives?

Central Party Leaders, General Secretary Xi, listen to this–how absurd are their remarks! We learn in middle school history books how the May 4th Movement was an extremely important event in China's modern contemporary history. It was an anti-imperialist, anti-feudalistic patriotic movement, the beginning of China's new democratic revolution; it led to the birth and development of the CCP. Peking University, one of the birthplaces of the May 4th Movement, has always been proud of this. When General Secretary Xi visited on May 2 this year, he emphasized to the whole university: "Today, in the midst of our Chinese nation's great journey to rejuvenation, Peking University teachers and students must continue to carry forward the spirit of the May 4th Movement, making new, even greater contributions to the nation, the country, and the people."

If you characterize our actions as forward progress, as us living the spirit of the May 4th Movement, then we can say without mincing words: "Yes!" But if you're going to accuse us of invoking the spirit of the May 4th Movement to stoke protests, to oppose the Party and socialism, if you accuse us of harboring unfathomable motives, if you simply equate the singing of the "Internationale" with engaging in color revolution, then we can never make this promise. Those who hold this opinion have completely forgotten the original values of the CCP and the People's Government. Could it be that the only reasonable course of action is to cover our own eyes, ignore society's suffering, and abandon the pursuit of fairness and justice? Is it truly the only right thing to do to violate the Constitution and oppress the working class alongside these evil forces?! See John Rudolph, "Detained Activist Yue Xin on the Jasic Workers," *China Digital Times*, August 24, 2018, https://chinadigitaltimes.net/2018/08/no-one-can-resist-the-tides-of-history-detained-activist-yue-xin-on-the-jasic-workers/.

Chapter Two

1. As reported in https://www.ourorient.com/the-warrior-spirit-of-china (accessed January 2019). Malraux was a French novelist, art theorist, and minister of cultural affairs. He is best known for his novel *La Condition Humaine* [Man's fate] (1933).

2. In addition to the military, other unclassified occupations in the Chinese context included the imperial clan, eunuchs, religious groups, entertainers, and slaves.

3. *A History of Chinese Civilization* (Cambridge: Cambridge University Press, 1982); originally published as *Le Monde Chinois* (Paris: Librarie Armand Colin, 1972).

4. Robert Eno, "Early Chinese Thought: Legalism and Huang-Lao Thought," 1, https://chinatxt.sitehost.iu.edu/Thought/Legalism.pdf.

5. Eno, "Early Chinese Thought. Li Si's ideas were codified in the writings of a prince of the state of Han, Han Feizi, in a book of the same name as its author, *Han Feizi*.

6. Included in this corpus are the *Six Secret Teachings*, *The Methods of Sima*, Sunzi's *Art of War*, the *Wuzi*, *Wei Laozi*, *Three Strategies of Huang Shigong*, and *Questions and Replies between Tang Taizong and Le Weigong*. See Ralph D. Sawyer and Mei Mei-chün Sawyer, *The Seven Military Classics of Ancient China* (Boulder, CO: Westview, 1993).

7. A statement attributed to Yelü Chucai (Mongolian, Urtu Saqal); Jerry Bentley, *Old World Encounters: Cross-Cultural Contacts and Exchanges in Pre-Modern Times* (New York: Oxford University Press, 1993), 143.

8. Ma Feibai, *Qín Shǐ Huángdì Zhuàn* (Nanjing: Jiangsu guji chubanshe, 1985; first published 1941).

9. Ma, *Qín Shǐ Huángdì Zhuàn*.

10. Hong Shidi's biography *Qin Shi Huang* (1972) initiated the reevaluation.

11. Referenced in Kenneth Lieberthal, Governing China, 1st ed. (New York: W.W. Norton and Company, 1995), 71.

12. Joyce C. H. Liu, "Paradoxical Routes of the Sinification of Marxism: Materialist Dialectic and Immanent Critique," in *East Asian Marxisms and Their Trajectories* (London: Taylor and Francis Group, 2017), 167 and 170.

13. Originally uttered by Mao during an emergency meeting of the CCP on August 7, 1927, at the beginning of the Chinese Civil War. Li Gucheng, ed., *A Glossary of Political Terms of the People's Republic of China* (Hong Kong: Chinese University Press, 1995), 325.

14. Sam Crane, "Why Xi Jinping's China is Legalist, Not Confucian," *Los Angeles Review of Books*, June 29, 2018.

15. Crane, "Why Xi Jinping's China is Legalist, Not Confucian."

16. Crane, "Why Xi Jinping's China is Legalist, Not Confucian."

17. Jianying Zha, "China's Heart of Darkness: Prince Han Fei & Chairman Xi Jinping," *China Heritage*, July 2020, https://chinaheritage.net/journal/chinas-heart-of-darkness-prince-han-fei-chairman-xi-jinping-prologue/.

18. "Politics under Xi Jinping: Centralization and its Implications," *Policy Research Institute, Ministry of Finance, Japan, Public Policy Review* 16, no. 3 (September 2020): 1–21.

Chapter Three

1. A good introduction remains Arthur Waley, *Three Ways of Thought in Ancient China* (Palo Alto, CA: Stanford University Press, 1939).

2. See *Confucius: The Secular as Sacred* (New York: Waveland, 1998).
3. *Daode jing* 38.
4. *Daode jing* 5.
5. For a comparison of over 175 translations of the opening chapter of the *Daode jing*, see http://www.bopsecrets.org/gateway/passages/tao-te-ching.htm
6. Daoism is indebted to the proto-Daoist tradition of the Yin and Yang School for its cosmological theory, whereby the primordial force of *Qi* (*yuanqi*) is divided into two complementary elements: *yang* (pure, light element; Heaven) and *yin* (dense, heavy element; Earth), which together produce the myriad things (human realm).
7. *Daode jing*, 2: "What is and what is not give birth to one another; What is difficult and what is easy complete one another; Long and short complement one another; High and low incline towards one another; Note and noise harmonize with one another; Before and after follow one another."
8. *Daode jing*, 2.
9. *Daode jing*, 2.
10. *Daode jing*, 28.
11. *Daode jing*, 4.
12. *Daode jing*, 8.
13. *Daode jing*, 11.
14. See Damian Carrington, "Humanity Has Wiped Out 60% of Animal Populations Since 1970," October 30, 2018, https://www.theguardian.com/environment/2018/oct/30/humanity-wiped-out-animals-since-1970-major-report-finds.
15. "Air Pollution Grows in Tandem with China's Economy," *NPR*, https://www.npr.org/2007/05/17/10221268/air-pollution-grows-in-tandem-with-chinas-economy (accessed January 21, 2021).
16. Melanie Hart and Jeffrey Cavanagh, "Environmental Standards Give the United States an Edge Over China." *Center for American Progress*, April 20, 2012, https://www.americanprogress.org/article/environmental-standards-give-the-united-states-an-edge-over-china/.
17. Ma Jun, "How Participation Can Help China's Ailing Environment." *ChinaDialogue*, January 31, 2007.
18. Rebecca Valli, "China Revises Economic Law," *VOA*, April 25, 2014, https://www.voanews.com/a/china-revises-environmental-law-to-address-pollution-problems/1900981.html.
19. James R. Ferguson, "China's Eco-Civilization: From History to Policy," in *A Discourse on Economic Development*, ed. K. Roy and C. Clark (New York: Nova Science, 2019), 87–118. For an introduction to the concept "Ecological Civilization (Civilisation)," see James Oswald, "China Turns to Ecology in Search of 'Civilisation,'" *Asian Studies Association of Australia*, 2016, http://asaa.asn.au/china-turns-to-ecology-in-search-of-civilisation/. On the tension between economic

expansion and ecological sustainability, see also Coraline Goron, "Ecological Civilisation and the Political Limits of a Chinese Concept of Sustainability," *China Perspectives* 4 (2018): 39–52; https://doi.org/10.4000/chinaperspectives.8463.

20. Teo Cheng Wee, "China Renews 'Green G.D.P.' Initiative," https://eponline.com/articles/2015/04/13/china-renews-green-gdp-initiative.aspx (accessed April 13, 2015).

21. "Mao Mountain Journal: China's Religious Revival Fuels Environmental Activism," *The New York Times*, July 12, 2017.

22. "Mao Mountain Journal."

23. "Mao Mountain Journal."

24. Murray Scot Tanner, "China Rethinks Unrest," *Washington Quarterly* 27, no. 3 (Summer 2004): 137–56. "Mass group incidents" are defined as "planned or impromptu gathering that forms because of internal contradictions," and can include public speeches or demonstrations, physical clashes, public airings of grievances, and other group behaviors that are seen as disrupting social stability (see Tao Ran, "China's Land Grab Is Undermining Grassroots Democracy," *Guardian*, December 16, 2011.

25. *Economist*, "Protest in China: The Cauldron Boils," September 29, 2005.

26. Michael Forsythe, "China's Spending on Internal Police Force in 2010 Outstrips Defense Budget," *Bloomberg*, March 6, 2011, https://www.bloomberg.com/news/articles/2011-03-06/china-s-spending-on-internal-police-force-in-2010-outstrips-defense-budget.

27. David Shambaugh, *China's Communist Party: Atrophy and Adaptation* (Washington, DC: Woodrow Wilson Center, 2008), 32.

28. Theresa Wright, *Accepting Authoritarianism: State-Society Relations in China's Reform Era* (Stanford, CA: Stanford University Press, 2010).

29. Xiabing Li, *A History of the Modern Chinese Army* (Lexington: University Press of Kentucky, 2007).

Chapter Four

1. Kenneth Rexroth, *One Hundred Poems from the Chinese* (New York: New Directions, 1971), 60.

2. On Yongming Yanshou's life, see Albert Welter, "Yongming Yanshou and the Complexities of Chan Identity," in *Yongming Yanshou's Conception of Chan in the* Zongjing Lu: *A Special Transmission within the Scriptures*, ed. Albert Welter (Oxford: Oxford University Press, 2011), 11–43.

3. Modeled after Xiaomei Zhao's report, "The Leshan Giant Buddha Scenic Area," *International Institute for Asian Studies Newsletter* 75 (2016): 8–9.

4. According to the latest survey data available from 2010, https://www.pewforum.org/2012/12/18/global-religious-landscape-buddhist/.

5. "The Red, Black and Gray Markets of Religion in China," *Sociological Quarterly* 47, no. 1 (2006): 93–122, http://doi.org/10.1111/j.1533-8525.2006.00039.x.

6. *Buddhism in Chinese Society: An Economic History from the Fifth to the Tenth Centuries*, translated by Franciscus Verellen (New York: Columbia University Press, 1995); originally published as *Les aspects économiques du bouddhisme dans la société chinoise du Ve au Xe siècle* (Saigon: École Francaise d'Extrême-Orient, 1956), 4.

7. Gregory V. Raymond, "Religion as a Tool of Influence: Buddhism and China's Belt and Road Initiative in Mainland Southeast Asia," *Contemporary Southeast Asia* 42, no. 3 (2020): 346–71.

8. Hangzhou Buddhist College, China Wiki, https://www.chinawiki.net/thread/48/27270.html.

Chapter Five

1. Welter, *Yongming Yanshou's Conception of Chan in the Zongjing lu* (New York: Oxford University Press, 2011), 211.

2. A connection first made by the Japanese scholar, Araki Kengo, *Bykkyō to Jukyō* (Buddhism and Confucianism) (Kyoto: Heirakuji shoten, 1972).

3. "Modernity and the Problem of Meaning: The Durkheimian Tradition." *Sociological Analysis* 46, no. 2 (1985): 109–30.

4. "Indigenous Epistemologies in the Age of Globalization," in Juan Poblete, ed., *Critical Latin American and Latino Studies* (Minneapolis: University of Minnesota Press, 2003), 139.

5. Cary Nederman, *Stanford Encyclopedia of Philosophy* (2014); https://plato.stanford.edu/entries/machiavelli/.

6. *International Herald Tribune*, 9–10 November 1991; cited in Daniel Bell entry on "Communitarianism" in the *Standard Encyclopedia of Philosophy* (revised edition, 2009), http://plato.stanford.edu/entries/communitarianism/index.html#note-5.

7. See, for example, the explanation of the Chinese position given by Liu Huaqiu, former vice-minister of foreign affairs, in his remarks to the United Nations World Conference on Human Rights in Vienna (June 1993): "The concept of human rights is a product of historical development. It is closely associated with specific social, political, and economic conditions and the specific history, culture, and values of a particular country. Different historical development stages have different human rights requirements. Countries at different development stages or with different historical traditions and cultural

backgrounds also have different understanding and practice of human rights. Thus, one should not and cannot think of the human rights standard and model of certain countries as the only proper ones and demand all countries to comply with them." See Vienna Conference Statement, 1993; cited in Stephen Angle, *Human Rights and Chinese Thought: A Cross-Cultural Inquiry* (Cambridge: Cambridge University Press, 2002), 1.

    8. See Sam Crane, "Why Xi Jinping's China is Legalist, Not Confucian" https://chinachannel.org/2018/06/29/legalism/; and Ryan Mitchell, "Is 'China's Machiavelli' Now Its Most Important Political Philosopher?," https://thediplomat.com/2015/01/is-chinas-machiavelli-now-its-most-important-political-philosopher/.

    9. Jiang Qing, "From Mind Confucianism to Political Confucianism," in *The Renaissance of Confucianism in Contemporary China*, ed. Ruiping Fan (New York: Springer, 2011).

    10. Welter, *The Administration of Buddhism in China: A Study and Translation of Zanning and his Topical Compendium of the Buddhist Order in China* (Da Song Seng shilue 大宋僧史) (Amherst, NY: Cambria, 2018).

Concluding Reflections

    1. *The Economist*, "Democracy Continues Its Disturbing Retreat," January 1, 2018, https://www.economist.com/graphic-detail/2018/01/31/democracy-continues-its-disturbing-retreat.

    2. Freedom House, "Democracy in Crisis: Freedom House Releases Freedom in the World 2108," January 15, 2017, https://freedomhouse.org/article/democracy-crisis-freedom-house-releases-freedom-world-2018.

    3. Viola Gienger, "In 2019, Will the Global March of Authoritarianism Turn into a Stampede or a Slog?," *Just Security* (website), January 14, 2019, https://www.justsecurity.org/62231/2019-global-march-authoritarianism-turn-stampede-slog/ (accessed February 2020).

    4. For background and assessment of BRI, see Andrew Chatzky and James McBride, Council on Foreign Relations, https://www.cfr.org/backgrounder/chinas-massive-belt-and-road-initiative (accessed February 2020).

    5. Bethany Allen-Ebrahimian, "A China-centric 21st Century," *Axios* (website), February 5, 2020, https://www.axios.com/china-xi-jinping-world-power-ab889b35-b5de-4e9b-b6a4-95e1c0110773.html.

    6. Allen-Ebrahimian, "A China-centric 21st Century."

    7. Bethany Allen-Ebrahimian, "Davos Leaders Don't Know How to Deal with China's Economic System," *Axios* (website), January 25, 2020, https://www.axios.com/davos-china-authoritarian-capitalism-e2bc7148-195a-4934-8f59-a6537a8bdf24.html?utm_source=flipboard&utm_medium=social&utm_campaign=cpdavos2020&utm_content=1100.

8. A cursory glance at https://en.wikipedia.org/wiki/List_of_Chinese_inventions underscores this point. For more sustained analysis, see Joseph Needham's ground-breaking, *Science and Civilisation in China*, 7 vols. (Cambridge: Cambridge University Press, 1954–2004).

9. *Lun yu* (*Analects*) 7.1.

10. *Li ji* (Book of Rites) *juan* 11, section 19.

11. Valerie Hansen, *The Open Empire, A History of China through 1600* (New York: W.W. Norton, 2000).

Epilogue

1. "Viral Alarm: When Fury Overcomes Fear," February 5, 2020, https://www.chinafile.com/reporting-opinion/viewpoint/viral-alarm-when-fury-overcomes-fear.

2. China Heritage, "Imminent Fears, Immediate Hopes—A Beijing Jeremiad," August 9, 2021, http://chinaheritage.net/journal/imminent-fears-immediate-hopes-a-beijing-jeremiad/.

3. Emma Graham-Harrison, "'This May Be the Last Piece I Write': Prominent Xi Critic Has Internet Cut after House Arrest," *Guardian*, February 15, 2020, https://www.theguardian.com/world/2020/feb/15/xi-critic-professor-this-may-be-last-piece-i-write-words-ring-true.

4. Translated and Annotated by Geremie R. Barmé, https://www.chinafile.com/reporting-opinion/viewpoint/viral-alarm-when-fury-overcomes-fear; emphasis mine.

5. Shi Jiangtao, "China Should Stop US Decoupling at Any Cost, Even Humiliation, Ultranationalist Writer Warns," *South China Morning Post*, December 28, 2021.

Postscript

1. Jonathon Hall, *Ethnic Identity in Greek Antiquity* (Cambridge: Cambridge University Press, 1997), 32. As cited in Erica Fox Brindley, *Ancient China and the Yue: Perceptions and Identities on the Southern Frontiers. C. 400 BCE–50 CE* (Cambridge: Cambridge University Press, 2015), 6.

2. Frank Dikötter, *The Discourse of Race in Modern China* (Oxford and New York: Oxford University Press, 2015), 2.

3. Dikötter, *The Discourse of Race in Modern China*, 3–7.

4. *Shujing* (Book of history), "Tribute of Yu."

5. Summarized in two master works on Chinese Buddhism, Erik Zürcher's *The Buddhist Conquest of China* (Leiden: Brill, 2007; first published 1959), and

Kenneth Kuan Sheng. Ch'en's *The Chinese Transformation of Buddhism* (Princeton, NJ: Princeton University Press, 2016; originally published 1973).

6. Dikötter, *The Discourse of Race in Modern China*, 20.

7. For a review of Chinese attitudes toward race in the modern period, see Dikötter, *The Discourse of Race in Modern China*, which is devoted to the development and evolution of these attitudes.

8. Human Rights Foundation Report, "100 Years of Suppression: The CCP's Strategies in Tibet, The Uyghur Region, and Hong Kong," 2021, https://hrf.org/wp-content/uploads/2021/08/CCP-REPORT-FINAL-VERSION.pdf.

Further Reading

On China's Rise

Ferguson, R. James, and Rosita Dellios. *The Politics and Philosophy of Chinese Power: The Timeless and the Timely.* Lanham, MD: Lexington, 2017.
Toje, Asle. *Will China's Rise Be Peaceful? The Rise of a Great Power in Theory, History, Politics, and the Future.* New York: Oxford University Press, 2018.
Xu, Jilin. *Rethinking China's Rise: A Liberal Critique.* Cambridge: Cambridge University Press, 2018.
Yee, Herbert S. *China's Rise: Threat or Opportunity?* Abingdon, Oxon: Routledge, 2011.

On the Revival of Confucianism

Bell, Daniel. *China's New Confucianism: Politics and Everyday Life in a Changing Society.* Princeton, NJ: Princeton University Press, 2010.
Bell, Daniel A., and Hahm Chaibong, eds. *Confucianism for the Modern World.* Cambridge: Cambridge University Press, 2003.
Billioud, Sébastien. *The Varieties of Confucian Experience: Documenting a Grassroots Revival of Tradition.* Leiden: Brill, 2018.
Billioud, Sébastien, and Joël Thoraval. *The Sage and the People: the Confucian Revival in China.* New York and Oxford: Oxford University Press, 2015.
Fingarette, Herbert. *Confucius: The Secular as Sacred.* Prospect Heights, IL: Waveland, 1998.
Hammond, Kenneth J., and Jeffrey L. Richie, eds. *The Sage Returns: Confucian Revival in Contemporary China.* Albany: State University of New York Press, 2015.

Makeham, John. *Lost Soul: "Confucianism" in Contemporary Chinese Academic Discourse*. Cambridge, MA: Harvard University Press, Harvard-Yenching Institute Monograph Series 64, 2008.

Makeham, John, ed. *New Confucianism: A Critical Examination*. London: Palgrave Macmillan, 2003.

Tamney, Joseph B., and Fenggang Yang, eds. *Confucianism and Spiritual Traditions in Modern China and Beyond*. Leiden: Brill, 2012.

On the Revival of Buddhism

Carter, James. *Heart of Buddha, Heart of China: The Life of Taixu, a Twentieth Century Monk*. New York and Oxford: Oxford University Press, 2011.

Kiely, Jan, and J. Brooks Jessup, eds. *Recovering Buddhism in Modern China*. New York: Columbia University Press, 2016.

Ritzinger, Justin R. *Anarchy in the Pure Land: Reinventing the Cult of Maitreya in Modern Chinese Buddhism*. New York and Oxford: Oxford University Press, 2017.

Welter, Albert. *A Tale of Two Stūpas: Diverging Paths in the Revival of Buddhism in Hangzhou China*. New York and Oxford: Oxford University Press, 2022.

Zhe, Ji, Gareth Fisher, and André Laliberté. *Buddhism after Mao: Negotiations, Continuities, and Reinventions*. Honolulu: University of Hawai'i Press, 2019.

On the Revival of Daoism

Dean, Kenneth. *Taoist Ritual and Popular Cults of Southeast China*. Princeton, NJ: Princeton University Press, 1993.

Palmer, David A., and Xun Liu, eds. *Daoism in the Twentieth Century: Between Eternity and Modernity*. Berkeley: University of California Press, 2012.

Schipper, Kristofer. *The Taoist Body*. Berkeley: University of California Press, 1994.

On the Revival of Chinese Culture

Dirlik, Arif. *Culture and History in Postrevolutionary China*. Hong Kong: Chinese University of Hong Kong Press, 2011.

Wang, Yuan-kang. *Harmony and War: Confucian Culture and Chinese Power Politics*. New York: Columbia University Press, 2010.

Yucao, Tian, Xueping Zhong, and Kebin Liao, eds. *Culture and Social Transformations in Reform Era China*. Leiden: Brill, 2010.

On the Revival of Religion in China

Chau, Adam Yuet. *Religion in Contemporary China: Revitalization and Innovation*. Milton Park, Abingdon-on-Thames, UK: Routledge, 2011.

DuBois, Thomas David. *Religion and the Making of Modern East Asia*. Cambridge, UK: Cambridge University Press, 2011.

Goossaert, Vincent, and David A. Palmer. *The Religious Question in Modern China*. Chicago: University of Chicago Press, 2012.

Goossaert, Vincent, Jan Kiely, and John Lagerwey, eds. *Modern Chinese Religion. II, 1850–2015*. Leiden: Brill, 2015.

Kuo, Cheng-tian, ed. *Religion and Nationalism in Chinese Societies*. Amsterdam: Amsterdam University Press, 2017.

On Race/Racism

Brindley, Erica. *Ancient China and the Yue: Perceptions and Identities on the Southern Frontier, c.400 BCE–50 CE*. Cambridge UK: Cambridge University Press, 2015.

Dikötter, Frank. *The Discourse of Race in Modern China*. Oxford and New York: Oxford University Press, 2015.

Xiang, Shuchen. "The Ghostly Other: Understanding Racism from Confucian and Enlightenment Models of Subjectivity." *Asian Philosophy* 25, no. 4 (2015): 384–401.

Xiang, Shuchen. "Why the Confucians Had No Concept of Race (Part I): The Anti-Essentialist Cultural Understanding of Self." *Philosophy Compass* 14, no. 10 (2019): 1–11. https://doi.org/10.1111/phc3.12628.

Yang, Shao-yun. *The Way of the Barbarians: Redrawing Ethnic Boundaries in Tang and Song China*. Seattle: University of Washington Press, 2019.

Index

Note: Page numbers in *italics* and **bold** indicate figures and tables, respectively, and page numbers following "n" refer notes.

#MeToo movement of China, 39

Abbot Yang, 69
actionless action. See *wuwei* (non-action)
Allen-Ebrahimian, Bethany, 123
Allison, Graham, 11
American Dream, 126
Analects (book of Confucian thoughts), 20–23, 27, 60
anti-Buddhism, 136. See also Buddhism
"applied *qi*," 63
The Art of War (Sun Tzu), 11, 14, 43, 45
Asian Infrastructure Investment Bank (AIIB) 4, 139n5
Autry, Greg, 12

Belt and Road Initiative (BRI) 4, 73, 98, 123–24, 139n4
Berthrong, John, 18
Biden, Joe, 122
Bin Song, 19
Book of Rites (Confucius), 125
"Boston Confucians," 13–14, 18–19; Boston University Confucian Association, 19; initiatives of, 19, 20; ritual veneration ceremony for Confucius, 19, *20*
Bo Xilai, 37, 38
Bo Yibo, 37
Budai Maitreya, 94; hall, 92; statue at Xuedou Monastery, 92–93, *93*
Buddhism, 7, 10, 15, 81, 134; China's use of, 23, 98–99; color designations of, 97; Confucianism *vs.*, 75–79; Cultural Revolution against, 79–80; growth and future in China, 95–99; Han elite in, 135–36; material and economic criteria, 97–98; struggles in Song dynasty, 105; as supports for ruler, 113–15
Buddhist Association of China, 98
Buddhist Noble Eightfold Path, 77
Buddhist revival in contemporary China, 75, 79; Four Great Persecutions, 80–81; Great Proletarian Cultural Revolution, 82; in Hangzhou, 82–83, 95; Leifeng Pagoda, 85–87, 89–91; Lingyin Monastery, 91–92;

Buddhist revival in contemporary China *(continued)*
Pattern of Buddhist Suppressions and, 81–82; role of monuments, 83–84; Xuedou Monastery, 92–95; Yongming Stūpa Hall, 87–89, 88; in Zhejiang province, 95

Bully of Asia: Why China's Dream is the New Threat to World Order (Mosher), 12

bureaucratic cycle" in China, 49, 54

CCP. *See* Chinese Communist Party
Center for American Progress, 67
Chang, Gordon C., 12
Charter 08 manifesto, 28
Chen Duxiu, 26
China: becoming ecological civilization, 8, 68; BRI, 123–24; "China Threat" in Contemporary Discourse, 11–13; COVID-19 pandemic impact, 129; cultural reinvention, 13; cyclical change in culture, 5–6; decline of Marxist ideology in, 35, 36; economic and political order, 4–5; economic prosperity, 130–31; economic resurgence in, 1, 122–23, 125; emergence of Communism in, 9, 26–27, 36–37, 93, 102, 114; innovations in, 125–26; Jesuit scholarship on, 140n6; liberalism and tolerance in, 28; "mandate of Heaven" concept, 5, 45–46; Marxism in, 120–21; modernity, 3, 6–7; and new world order, 8, 9–11; paradigm shifts in, 113–14; preservation of tradition, 125; race and ethnicity in, 133–34; reinvention of contemporary cultural identity, 9; role in climate change, 7–8; role of militarism in, 45; Self-Strengthening Movement of, 2; six arts of, 42–43; socialism with Chinese characteristics, 125, 127; *ti* and *yong* model, 1–2, 3–4

Chinese authoritarianism, 121, 122; dynastic cycle in, 45–50; Legalism of Xi Jinping, 54–57; modern China, dynastic cycle and, 50–54

Chinese Communist Party (CCP), 7, 8, 24, 26–27, 71, 74; authoritarian model of socialism, 117, *117*; Buddhist "soft power" utilized by, 98; and Confucianism, 37; evolving as one-party state, 131–32; generational transitions in 51; structure of authority in, 115, *116*; Wang Lijun incident, 38–39; Yue Xin's issue, 39–40

"Chinese Dream," 11–12, 68, 126, 137

Chinese New Left, 38
Chongqing model, 37–38
Christianity, 75, 99, 118
"Come to Confucius" moment, 20
The Coming Collapse of China (Chang), 12
Communism in China, 9, 26–27, 36–37, 93, 102, 114
Communist Party in China. *See* Chinese Communist Party (CCP)
Confucian(s), 106–7; altruism 21; Confucian-Marxist leadership, 54; exclusivism and exceptionalism, 24; external system," 109; program of Great Learning, 77
Confucianism, 7, 8, 15, 59, 61, 81, 96; *vs.* Buddhism, 75–79; CCP's revolt against, 24; classical, 23, 105, 107, 114, 134; and "complex of modernity," 106–7; Confucian models and agendas, 107–9; decline in China, 26–28;

dimensions of political legitimacy, 111–13; Emperor Wu's promotion of, 42; fundamental values of, 21–22; Han elite in, 134–35; history of, 23–24; ideal of four classes, 41, 42; impact in other regions of East Asia, 22; Legalism links to, 44–45, 50; "mandate of Heaven" concept, 5, 45–46; Mind Confucianism, 109–10; in modern China, 52; moral virtues, 59–60; Political Confucianism, 109, 110–11; pro-Confucian initiative of Xi Jinping, 32–34; revival in China, 7, 10, 23, 29, 82, 101–2, 118; in Song dynasty, 103–6; as supports for ruler, 113–15; third iteration of Confucian tradition, 102–3; tied to authoritarianism, 117; Xi Jinping's promotion of, 34–40; See also Daoism; Legalism
Confucius: The Secular as Sacred (Fingarette), 14, 19
Confucius, 7, 17, 21, 75, 101, 125; Fingarette's views about, 19, 20–21; Mao's vilification of, 24, 31–32; Neo-Confucian interpretation of, 22; rehabilitation of, 29; statue at Tiananmen Square, 29, 30, 31; veneration at Boston University, 20
Crane, Sam, 35, 54, 55, 108
"Criticize Confucius" campaign, 27
Crouching Tiger: What China's Militarism Means for the World (Chang), 12
Cultural Revolution in China, 27–28, 38, 53, 79–80, 82, 131
Cyberspace Information Office, 57

Dao-jia (Family of the Dao), 70
Dao-jiao (Teaching of the Dao), 70

dao (Way), 61–66, 69, 77; "applied *qi*," 63; *Dao/dao* distinction, 63; "eternal *Dao*," 63; ineffability of, 65–66; workings of, 63–65, 65; *See also* Daoism
Daode jing (classic on the way and its virtue), 61–66, 70, 145n7
Daoism, 7, 10, 14, 59, 81, 145n6; associations with "superstition," 117, 118; "Green Dao" in Contemporary China, 66–70; Han elite in, 135; religious Daoism as revolutionary force, 70–74; struggle in Song dynasty, 105; as supports for ruler, 113–15; *See also* Confucianism; Legalism
de (as power of individuation) concept in Daoism, 64, 65
Death by China: Confronting the Dragon—A Global Call to Action (Navarro and Autry), 12
Deng Xiaoping, 26–28, 35, 53, 72, 120–22; capitalist market reforms, 35, 36; moderate governance of, 131
Destined for War: Can America and China Escape Thucydides's Trap? (Allison), 11
devout laity, 91
Doctrinal Buddhist literati, 104
dynastic cycle in China, 47, 48, 54, 71–72; interplay between Confucianism and Legalism, 45–50; and modern China, 50–54

ecological civilization (*shengtai wenming*), 8, 68
essence/function (*ti/yong*) matrix, 17–18
"eternal *Dao*," 63
ethnicity in Chinese culture, 133–34

158 | Index

Examining Legalist Theories and Censuring Confucianism movement, 53

Falun Gong (spiritual practice), 96
Fat Buddha. See Budai Maitreya
Ferguson, R. James, 68
filial piety, 21, 22
Fingarette, Herbert, 14, 19, 20, 22–24, 60
Five Hundred Arhats Hall, 92
Four Great Persecutions, 80–81
"Four Olds," 27–28, 79

Gardels, Nathan, 33
Gernet, Jacques, 44, 97
Gienger, Viola, 122
Gong, Falun, 72
"grand strategy of three teachings," 114–15
"great harmony" (datong), 133–34
"great hero" hypothesis, 47, 48, 49
Great Proletarian Cultural Revolution, 27, 82
"Green Dao" environmental movements in China, 14, 66–70
Guangdong model, 39
Guofeng, Hua, 28
guwen perspective, 104, 105

Hall, Jonathan, 133
Han Feizi, 55, 56
Han (hanhua) superiority, 134–36
Han Yu, 75–76, 103
Hangzhou Buddhist Academy, 99
hanhua Buddhism, 136
"Harmonious Society" (hexie shehui), 40
Holstein, William J., 11
House of National Continuity, 112, 113
House of Plebeians, 112, 113

House of Profound Confucians, 112, 113
House Sayings of Confucius (Kongzi jiayu), 34
Hsü, C. Y., 25
Hu Jintao, 28, 33, 53, 120, 131
Hu Shi, 26
Huang Fei, 85
Huangfei Pagoda. See Leifeng (Thunder peak) Pagoda
Huang-Lao Dao, 71
humaneness (ren), 21, 59–60
human rights, 147–48n7
Hundred-Year Marathon: China's Secret Strategy to Replace America as the Global Superpower (Pillsbury), 11–12
Hundred Schools of Thought of the Spring and Autumn and Warring States periods, 59

Indian Buddhist culture, 83–84
"inner sagehood" (neisheng), 17–18
"inner sagehood/outer kingship" (neisheng/waiwang) distinction, 17
"Intellectual Awakening," 25
Islam, 10, 99

Jacques, Martin, 12, 13
Japan: "Eastern ethics/morality, Western technical learning" model, 1, 2; in economic and political world order, 4–5; economic stagnation, 4
Japan as Number One (Vogel), 4
JASIC Workers Solidarity Group, 39
Jesuit scholarship on China, 140n6
Jiabao, Wen, 67
Jiang Qing, 53, 109; Mind Confucianism of, 109–10; Political Confucianism of, 109, 110–11;

proposal for tri-cameral legislature, 111–13
Jiang Shigong, 54–55
Jiang Zemin, 28, 53, 120, 131
Jianjun, Jiangxi Li, 29
Jin dynasty, 136
jingzuo (quiet sitting), 105
junzi ("Cultured Person" or "Superior Person"), 59–60, 78

Kai-shek, Chiang, 30, 52, 71, 92
Kailai, Gu, 38
Kant, Immanuel, 3
Kazuko Kojima, 56
King Aśoka stūpa in Ningbo, 85; from Leifeng Pagoda ruins, 86; minted by King Qian Chu, 87
Kingly Way (*wangdao*), Confucian vision of, 111–13
Kissinger, Henry, 13
Konan, Naitō, 103

Lao-Tzu monumental statue at Mt. Qingyuan, 70
Laughing Buddha. *See* Budai Maitreya
Lee Kwan Yu, 106, 121, 127
Legalism, 12, 14, 40, 43–44, 59–61; institution of administrative measures, 44; links to Confucianism, 44–45, 50; tied to authoritarianism, 117, 138; Xi Jinping and, 54–57; *See also* Confucianism; Daoism
Leifeng Pagoda, 85–86, 89, 91; King Aśoka style stūpa from, 86, 87; stakeholders, 89–90, 90
Li Si, 45
Li Zehou, 3
Lin Biao, 28
Lingyin Monastery, 91–92
Liu Huaqiu, 147n7

Liu Xiaobo, 28
Lu Xun, 87
Lunyu. *See Analects*

Machiavelli, Niccolò, 44, 106
Ma Jun, 67
Malraux, Andre, 41
"mandate of Heaven" concept, 5, 45–46, 47–48
Mao Yuanxin, 32
Mao Zedong, 26, 27, 29, 30, 51, 53, 71, 79, 122, 131; attention to declining legacy of, 29; eliminating Confucianism from China, 26–28; vilification of Confucius, 24, 31–32
Marxism in China, 35, 36, 120–21
Marx, Karl, 3
May Fourth movement, 26, 36, 142–43n37
Mencius, 45, 73
Mind Confucianism, 109–10
Mind-Nature Confucianism. *See* Mind Confucianism
Mosher, Steven, 12
Mou Zongsan, 13, 17–18

Navarro, Peter, 12
neisheng issue, 110
Neo-Confucianism, 22–24, 77–78, 105–6, 108–9, 114, 118, 140n7. *See also* Confucianism
Neville, Robert, 18
The New Art of War: China's Deep Strategy Inside the United States (Holstein), 11
"New Confucian" (*dangdai xin rujia*) movement, 17, 23
New Confucianism, 13, 24, 55, 105, 109, 118. *See also* Confucianism
New Culture movement, 24–25, 37, 101, 131; liberal democratic ideals and impulses of, 28–29; reappraisals

New Culture movement (continued)
and divisions, 26; rejection of, 36; renunciation of Confucian culture, 31; stages of, 25

On China (Kissinger), 13
"outer kingship" (waiwang), 17–18

Paris Peace Conference, 25–26
Peking University, 143n37
People's Liberation Army (PLA), 73
Pew Research Center, 95
"Philosophical Daoism," 71
Pillsbury, Michael, 11
PLA. See People's Liberation Army
Political Confucianism, 109, 110–11
Polo, Marco, 83
PRC. See People's Republic of China
Putin, Vladimir, 121

Qi (yuanqi), 145n6
Qian Chu, 84, 87; stūpa, 85
Qiantang. See Hangzhou
Qin Shihuangdi, 42, 51–53, 57
Qing dynasty, 136

"Reform and Revolution" movement, 25
"remonstrances," 129
righteousness (yi), 21–22, 60
ritual propriety (li), 21, 59–60
Ruism, 103–4, 107
Ru tradition. See Ruism

Sakuma Shōzan, 1
Śākyamuni, 77, 92
Seidman, Steven, 106
"Self-Strengthening" movement, 2, 25, 36, 37
Seven Military Classics, 45
Shang Yang, 55

Shanghai Cooperation Organization (SCO) 4, 139n6
Sinicized Buddhism, 117
Sinicized Islam, 117
Song dynasty, 103; guwen perspective in, 104, 105; Neo-Confucians in, 118; race and ethnicity in, 136; responses to creating wen models in, 104; Ru tradition in, 103–4, 105; wen culture in, 104, 105
Song xue (Song Learning) movement, 103
"son of Heaven" concept, 47
state-sponsored capitalism, 6
Sun Tzu, 11, 14, 43, 45
Sunzi. See Sun Tzu

Taiping movements, 71, 82
Tang-Song transition, 103
Tiananmen Square: democracy movement in, 131; Mao's picture in, 29, 30, 31; National Museum, 31; protests, 3, 71; statue of Confucius at, 29, 30, 31
ti and yong (essence and function) model of China, 1–2, 3–4
tianxia (all under Heaven), 133
Tibetan Buddhism, 99
traditional advocates of Buddhist teachings, 104
Travels (Marco Polo), 83
Treaty of Versailles. See Paris Peace Conference
tri-cameral legislature of Qing, 111, 112
Trump, Donald, 11, 122
Tu Wei-ming, 13, 18
Twenty-One Demands, 24

Varese, Stefano, 106
Vogel, Ezra, 4

Wang, Abbot, 69
Wang Xiaodong, 132
Wang Xuedian, 33
wangdao concept, 112
Wang Lijun incident, 38–39
"War against Chinese Expansionism," 73
wen (literary culture), 103–5, **104**
When China Rules the World: The End of the Western World and the Birth of a New Global Order (Jacques), 12–13
World Buddhist Forums, 98
wu (martial prowess), 103; to *wen* transition of Chinese dynasty, 46–47, 49
wuwei (non-action), 62, 64, 66
Wuyue kingdom, 84
Wuzi, 45

Xi Jinping, 11, 14, 32, 50–54, 72, 94, 113, 120, 126, 129, 130; authoritarian rule of, 121, 140n11; BRI initiative, 123; diplomacy strategy, 139n4; encouraging "socialism with Chinese characteristics," 117; initiatives to increase CCP morale, 96; Legalism of, 54–57; and May 4th Movement, 142–43n37; pro-Confucian initiative, 32–34; promotion of Confucianism, 34–40, 108
Xi Jinping: How to Read Confucius and Other Chinese Classical Thinkers, 34
xinxing ruxue,. See Mind Confucianism
Xu Zhangrun, 129–30
Xuedou Monastery, 92–95
Xunzi, 44–45, 52, 56, 111

YCP. *See* Young Communist Party
yin and *yang* matrix, 61, 62, 145n6
Yongming Monastery, 87
Yongming Stūpa Hall, 87–89, 88
Yongming Yanshou, 87–88
Young Communist Party (YCP), 26
Yu Ying-shih, 3
Yuan dynasty, 136
Yue Xin, 39–40

Zanning, 114; "grand strategy of three teachings," 114–15; suggestion of Ding vessel, 115, 116
Zhejiang Archaeological Association, 90
Zhou Enlai, 26
Zhu Xi, 103, 105
Zongmi, 105
zuochan (sitting meditation), 105

www.ingramcontent.com/pod-product-compliance
Lightning Source LLC
Chambersburg PA
CBHW030828230426
43667CB00008B/1424